S0-CCG-195

GREAT MARQUES

GREAT MARQUES

Chris Harvey

General Editor
John Blunsden

CHARTWELL
BOOKS, INC.

Author's note

I was especially pleased when writing this book to be able to include the latest MG saloons. Had this publication been produced earlier it might have had a very sad ending with the apparent cessation of the marque when the famous old factory at Abingdon closed in 1980. However, there is now hope that the marque M.G. has a secure future with the introduction of the Metro, Maestro and Montego saloons.

My thanks especially to the man responsible for some of M.G.'s greatest glories, John Thornley, for his assistance and members of the club he helped to start, the M.G. Car Club (particularly secretary Peter Tipton) and to Roche Bentley, whose relatively new association, the M.G. Owners' Club, has engineered so much fresh enthusiasm at grass roots level; in the same context, I must also thank Clive Richardson of British Leyland and Anders Clausager of Leyland Heritage, and the photographers whose pictures make these books so special.

Where possible, owners and custodians of the cars, at the time of photography, are mentioned in the captions to the illustrations.

Chris Harvey

Special photography:
Ian Dawson and Chris Linton

ENDPAPERS AND PAGES 1-5 *1934 P A Midget*, provided by Roger F. Thomas.

This edition 1989

**Published by Chartwell Books, Inc.
A division of Book Sales, Inc.
110 Enterprise Avenue.
Secaucus, New Jersey 07094**

© Octopus Books Ltd 1985

ISBN: 1-55521-425-8

Produced by Mandarin Offset
Printed and bound in Hong Kong

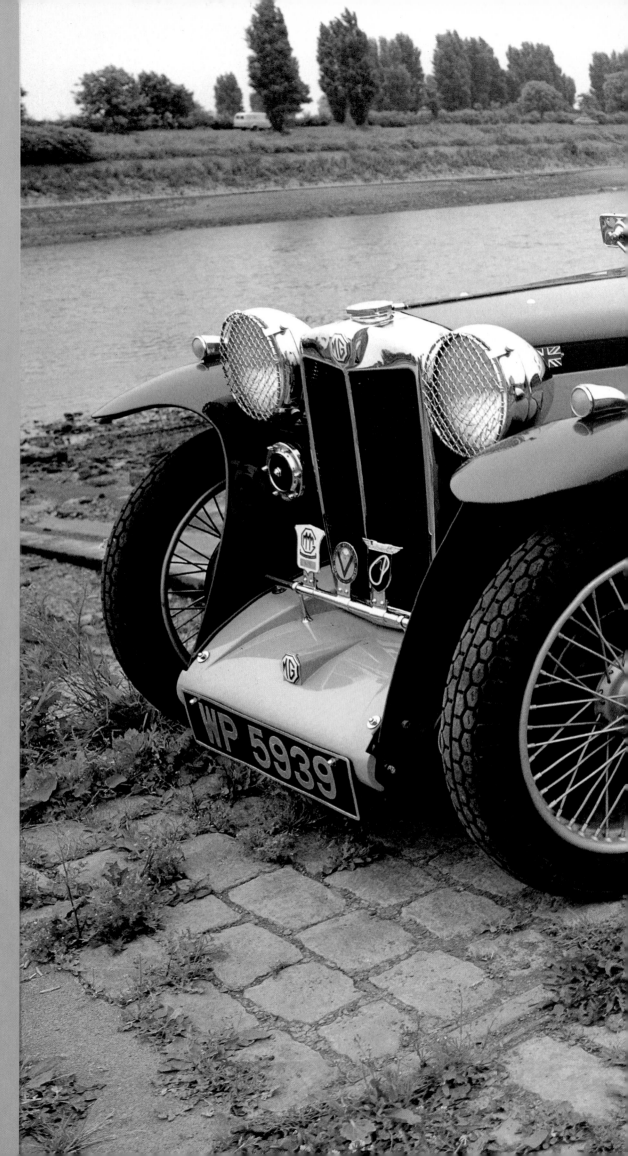

CONTENTS

From Bullnose to Midget

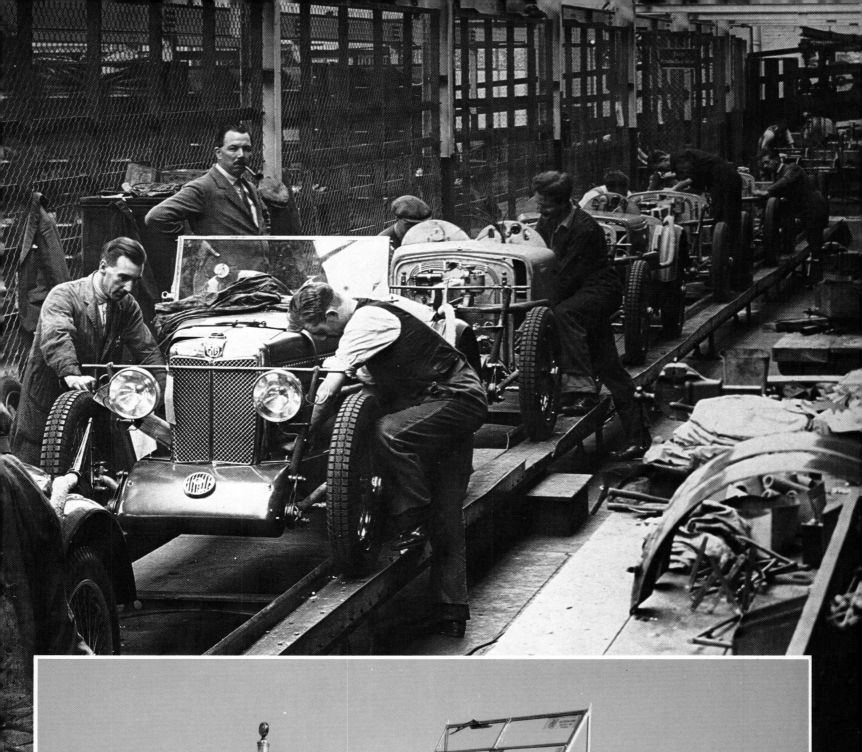

Seldom has any make of car aroused more emotion than M.G., emotion that has, above all, been fired by love. This is because M.G.s have always been cheap and cheerful sporting cars, dream machines that the ordinary man and woman could afford. These were cars you could depend on because they were built from rugged, well-tried components that started life in stolid saloons. But essentially they were vehicles that represented an escape from mundane life. They always looked like cars that raced on the track, and felt like them, which is the whole essence of sporting cars and why M.G.s – or MGs as they have been known since 1982 – have always been so popular.

The first M.G.s grew from the frustration felt by Cecil Kimber, manager of Morris Garages in Oxford, at having to sell the products of Morris Motors. These sturdy, but rather staid cars, distinguished by their 'bull-nosed' radiators, became very popular as their maker, William Morris, cut his prices dramatically during a period of great inflation. Kimber, a man of diverse talents, ranging from cost accountancy to writing and drawing, knew that he could sell Bullnose Morris cars for a higher price, and as a result make more profit on each vehicle, if he tuned them to go faster and fitted a more sporting body. It was a common practice at that time – in the early 1920s – for manufacturers' main agents, such as Morris Garages, to produce these sporting vehicles to cream greater profits from the top end of the market, and Kimber was uncommonly good at it.

The first cars that could be attributed to Kimber and Morris Garages were built in 1922. They used the chassis and running gear from the cheaper of the Bullnose cars, called the Cowley, and with special bodywork they sold for around the same price as the more fully equipped Oxford. Kimber's system was to order a standard Cowley chassis, lower the suspension, and have it fitted with a 'Chummy' body to his own design. This was an open two-seater with a space at the back for occasional passengers, rather like the modern 'two-plus-two' body styles. These cars were unusual in that the hood covered all the occupants, rather than just the two at the front, and were painted in pastel shades; they also had leather upholstery. They were far more sporting than anything Morris had attempted to make, and sold extremely well. At first they were produced in Oxford at the Longwall Street depot of Morris Garages, and were known as the Morris Garages Chummies. Early in 1923, production was transferred to a mews workshop to allow the Morris Garage fitters to carry on unhindered with their normal work of servicing Morris cars and preparing new vehicles for sale. One of the foremen, Cecil Cousins, and two other men worked as many as 80 hours a week, collecting chassis from the main Morris works at Cowley, near Oxford, modifying them at the new workshop in Alfred Lane, Oxford, delivering the chassis to the coachbuilders, Carbodies, collecting them, and finishing them off back at Alfred Lane. Incredibly, production was as many as 20 a week at one time!

Kimber, an enthusiastic sportsman with a flair for publicity, was keen to indulge in competition with one of his cars, so he had it tuned at Longwall Street, and in March 1923 won a gold medal in the classic London-to-Land's End Trial. Kimber exploited this success by ordering six two-seater bodies from Raworth of Oxford to be fitted to slightly modified Cowley chassis. These featured a raked windscreen, with scuttle ventilators like those on a yacht: it was no coincidence that boating was another of Kimber's interests. However, these were priced at twice the cost of a Morris Cowley, so sales were slow. But they were the first cars to be known as M.G.s, the full name of Morris Garages being thought rather cumbersome by Kimber.

At the same time, Morris Motors – stung into action by Kimber's success – introduced its own version of the Chummy at a lower price. With his base whipped from under him, Kimber first tried the Chummy body on a Morris Oxford chassis, and then a more powerful 14 hp engine as standard. As neither venture repeated the success of the Chummy, he therefore tried a better-finished saloon body on the Oxford chassis, called the 14/28 because of its new engine. But again, the price was too high at 15 per cent more than a standard Oxford saloon. It was, however, the first M.G. advertised as such. Various other models followed before Kimber started building 14/28 four-seaters, known as M.G. Specials, with lines following those of a glamorous and far more expensive contemporary, the Vauxhall 30/98. One of the first of these cars went to Billy Cooper, who helped keep times at the Brooklands track, and as such became a frequent, and much-admired, sight parked near the starting line of this celebrated prewar circuit.

PRECEDING PAGES *By 1931, when this photo was taken, Abingdon was well on the way to becoming the world's largest sports car factory. Already M.G. Midgets accounted for more than half the firm's total production, sporting saloons making up the rest. The small cars were produced in a variety of forms, these ones being competition versions known as the Montlhéry Midget.*

PRECEDING PAGES, INSET *The Super Sports, pictured here on display at Silverstone during an M.G. Car Club meeting, was one of the first true M.G.s, built in 1925 and based on the popular Bullnose Morris.*

'Old Number One' (1925)			
ENGINE		**CHASSIS**	
Type	11.9 hp Hotchkiss, in-line, water-cooled	Frame	Modified Morris Cowley, twin side members, cross members
No. of cylinders	4		
Bore/stroke mm	69.5 × 102	Wheelbase mm	2591
Displacement cc	1548	Track – front mm	1219
Valve operation	Overhead, pushrod	Track – rear mm	1219
Sparkplugs per cyl.	1	Suspension – front	Half-elliptic springs, beam axle
Compression ratio	5:1		
Induction	1 SU carburettor, air pressure fuel feed, hand pump	Suspension – rear	Half-elliptic springs, live axle
BHP	Approximately 35	Brakes	Morris Oxford drums front and rear
		Tyre size	710 × 90
DRIVE TRAIN		Wheels	Wire spoke
Clutch	Wet cork, single driven plate	**PERFORMANCE**	
Transmission	Three-speed manual gearbox	Maximum speed	129 km/h (80 mph)
		Acceleration	0-60 mph 20 sec
		Number built	1

RIGHT *Old Number One might have got its name as the result of a publicity foible, but it matters little: it was still one of the first true M.G.s. Provided by BL Heritage Limited.*

Octagons everywhere

It was also during this period, in the summer of 1924, that the M.G. motif appeared inside an octagon, the eight-sided symbol that was to become a trademark of M.G. Many devoted enthusiasts still make a point of signing letters to like-minded friends, 'Yours octagonally'.

In those early days, manufacturers still brought out new and revised models every year at the London Motor Show; and among the changes to the 1925 Morris Oxford was a longer wheelbase at 2740 mm (9 ft) rather than 2590 mm (8 ft 6 in). This gave the coachbuilders far more scope when they were making M.G. bodies, with the result that the four-seater tourer became one of the most beautiful cars of its day. The long lines were accentuated by a striking finish with the basic colour at the top and polished aluminium sides beneath. This was a highly unusual practice in 1925 and was probably inspired by the colour schemes used on boats. This lovely car – once described as a 'scaled-down Bentley at a third the price' – became an immediate best-seller and Kimber was

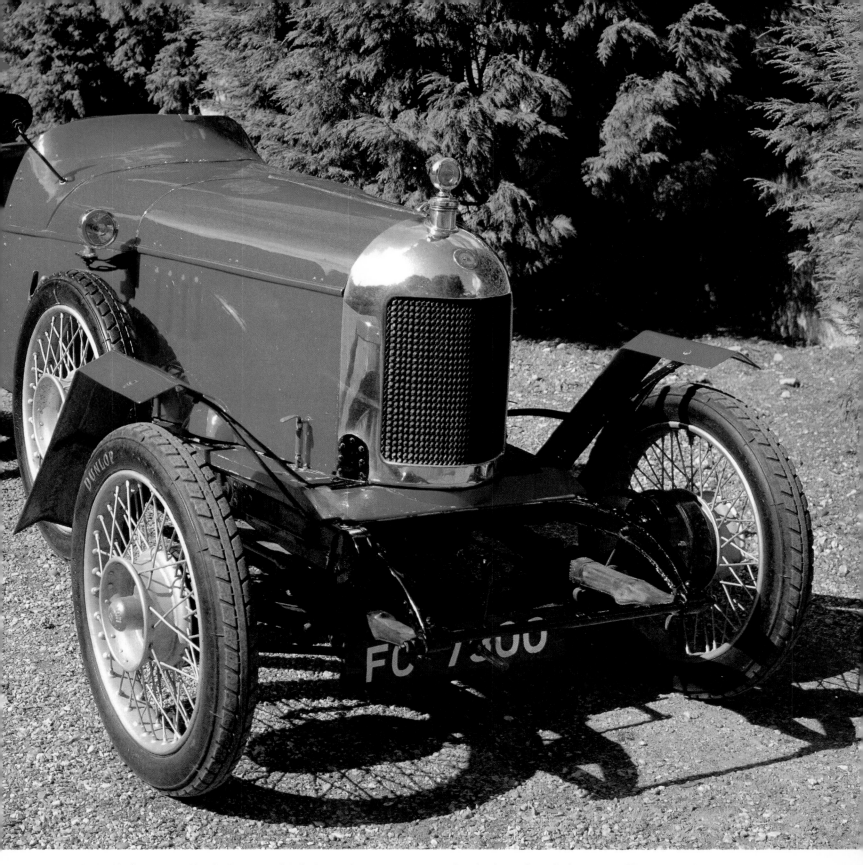

glad that he had insisted on calling it simply the M.G. Super Sports, dropping all reference to Morris in the title. After all, with its improved chassis and superb body, it bore little resemblance to its parent, sometimes described as the Model T Ford of Britain.

Alfred Lane was extremely busy all that year, producing 160 cars, mostly tourers, although there were a number of two-seaters and six Salonettes. The latter were a type of Grand Touring car of the 1920s, with a two-plus-two fixed-head body that fired Kimber with enthusiasm. Most of his customers preferred more conventional coachwork, however. It should be remembered that these M.G.s were still simply specials, because Morris topped the British sales that year with a figure of 54,000 vehicles!

Old Number One
The relentless march of William Morris swallowed up his suppliers, including Hotchkiss, the engine makers. This company's powerful

overhead valve unit really interested Kimber: during 1924 he had one fitted to a modified Cowley chassis and, early in 1925, it acquired a skimpy two-seater body. It was a pure competition special, and took him to another gold medal in the Land's End Trial that year, before being sold to a friend. That was the last the M.G. works saw of it – until it was rescued from a scrapyard by an M.G. employee in 1932 and returned to Abingdon in 1933. It was then restored to be used for demonstrations, before being heralded, by the Nuffield Organization (as William Morris's empire had become known in 1934) as 'The first M.G., built in 1923!' Not only was the date incorrect, but also it was not actually the first M.G.; nevertheless, it has been known ever since as Old Number One.

This car coincided, however, with the start of serious production, so perhaps the corporate publicists, who have since come in for considerable criticism for treating the sacred octagon's history in such a cavalier manner, were not committing such a serious crime. It is very difficult to pick an exact point when M.G.s stopped being simply modified Morris cars and became a great marque. Production expanded at such a rate in 1925, however, that the M.G. works was moved in September that year to the Morris Radiators factory in Bainton Road, Oxford, where there was more room. The M.G. range stabilized with sporting models (the open two-seater, open tourer and Salonette) on modified Oxford chassis, and special models (a landaulette, Weymann fabric-bodied sedan, and V-front saloon) on standard Oxford chassis. A talented Morris engineer, Hubert Charles, also became involved with Kimber at this point, helping with engine tuning and experimental work.

However, the next year, 1926, was a difficult one for M.G., as Morris revamped his cars along American lines. He replaced the bull-nosed radiator with a flat-fronted type and produced a much heavier and wider chassis, to allow more room inside the body. This was all very well, but it was the potential ruin of the M.G.'s lines, and the extra weight was a threat to its performance. Nevertheless, the workforce, an incredibly happy band of men, toiled all day and much of the night to make each M.G. Super Sports go as fast as the earlier model. Every engine was specially tuned and Kimber managed to retain enough of the previous elegance to ensure the body remained attractive. There was at least a bonus in that the heavier chassis was stiffer, making the car easier to handle. The engine was also considerably uprated to around 35 bhp during 1927, and subsequently all the flat-radiator models have become known as 14/40s rather than 14/28s. The 40 came from M.G.'s rather optimistic view of the engine's power output, a trend shared by many manufacturers at that time.

Sales continued to rise and another enforced move – to a brand-new factory in Edmund Road, Oxford – followed in September 1927 as more space was needed. Kimber continued to experiment with different body styles, offering a Featherweight Fabric Saloon and a fixed-head and drophead coupé. At this point, the M.G. works became more independent of Morris Motors, taking over responsibility from them for all work on M.G.s under guarantee – even if they did have Morris chassis and running gear – and adopting its own chassis numbers at the same time. This process of establishing the cars as a separate marque was carried to its logical conclusion when the M.G. Car Company was formed in 1928. The new firm, which like Morris Motors was owned personally by William Morris, started to issue its own handbooks, and Kimber went to great pains to emphasize M.G.'s individuality; this was more than justified by the amount of work that went into improving the Morris Oxford's engine and chassis, besides fitting different bodies. Octagons appeared all over the place – anywhere it was possible to recast a circular shape! – to proclaim the car's identity. If Kimber could have used octagonal wheels, he would have done so!

Enter the Midget
Meanwhile, William Morris's empire had continued to expand, greatly to the benefit of M.G., when he took over the bankrupt Wolseley concern in 1927. This company had developed a brilliant little 8 hp

overhead camshaft four-cylinder engine for a baby car that appealed to Morris because he wanted to produce a rival for the Austin Seven. However, this 847 cc Wolseley engine endowed a prototype Morris Minor with such a good performance that Morris decided to have it detuned for everyday use. Kimber got hold of one of the prototype cars, and quickly saw how it could be modified and rebodied in a similar way to the old Bullnose to produce a nippy little sports car.

At the same time, Hotchkiss – whose manager, Frank Woollard, was a good friend of Kimber's – produced an 18 hp overhead camshaft six-cylinder engine, ostensibly for a new Morris car. The resultant Isis turned out to be heavy and uninspiring, but Kimber saw it was a vehicle for his ambition to make a big sports car to match the best, namely Bentley. He designed a new chassis, and a cylinder block to take twin carburettors, and built what amounted to a completely new car, the 18/80 M.G. Six. This magnificent beast also bore a proud new radiator, which was so elegant that its essential shape survived on M.G.s for more than 25 years. The new small M.G., the Midget, was fitted with a scaled-down version of the radiator and, together with the 14/40, the two new models made their début at the 1928 London Motor Show.

The Midget, with a performance as good as the 14/40 at half the price, was an immediate success. The 18/80, at around half as much again as a 14/40, enjoyed more modest sales.

The move to Abingdon
During the year that followed, M.G. production figures tripled, with the M-type Midget, as the new small car was known, accounting for more than 50 per cent of the firm's total sales. The 18/80 was also quite popular, making up one third of the M.G. turnover; the 14/40 was about to be discontinued. Such was the volume of cars, around 1000, that the emergent M.G. Car Company had to move yet again in January 1930, to

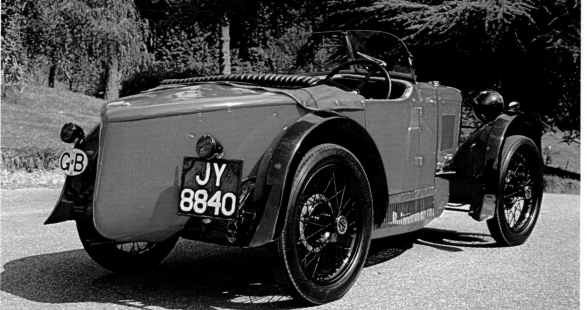

ABOVE *Building cars in the grand old manner at Abingdon in 1930 – chassis testers take out two examples of the 18/80, with its archetypal M.G. radiator, to find any faults before bodies are fitted.*

LEFT *Much of M.G.'s success was founded on the Midget. This 1930 M-type export model was fitted with metal panelling to withstand the ravishes of hot and sultry climates. Provided by Keith J. Portsmore.*

RIGHT *The F-type Magna of 1932 was a decidedly up-market model with a heavily disguised engine of Wolseley origin, and a longer wheelbase to help accommodate two extra seats under the tonneau cover. Wealthy owners included Prince Birabongse, the racing driver. Provided by Elwin S. Sapcote.*

Abingdon, 10 km (6 miles) from Oxford, but at least on the same side of the city as Cowley. This site, next to the disused Pavlova Leather Works, was to become the world's biggest sports car factory, distinguished by its brown-and-cream colour scheme (and octagonal embellishments!). It was also at this time that the enduring M.G. slogan 'Safety Fast' was coined.

Sales continued to soar because the overhead camshaft cars were such good performers in their price bracket, and naturally they soon became popular in competition as well – the subject of the next chapter. Not surprisingly, the needs of customers interested in competition started to influence the design of new M.G.s. During this period, the nucleus of Abingdon's formidable workforce was formed; it included Hubert Charles as Kimber's right-hand man on design, with Cecil Cousins and engine man Reg Jackson, and was reinforced by relative newcomers such as Gordon Phillips and Syd Enever, who provided outstanding talent on development. It was in 1930, too, that a young accountant, John Thornley, helped to start the M.G. Car Club, which was to become the world's biggest single-marque club. It was only natural that Thornley should join the M.G. staff in 1931, and it was a good job, too; eventually he was to take over Kimber's role as defender of the M.G. faith in the face of big business interests.

As the Midget continued to be an outstanding sales and competition success (it should be remembered that sports cars sell in far smaller numbers than family saloons and frequently provide a thorn in the flesh of the manufacturing moguls who want to standardize everything for maximum profits) the 18/80 was redesigned in far heavier Mark II guise to make it more of a Morris Motors flagship. However, the earlier 18/80, which became known as the Mark I, continued in production, and with the Midget provided the solid backbone of M.G. sales.

By this time, M.G.'s competition experiences were beginning to pay off, not only in sales, but in development. A new, longer-wheelbase chassis (2134 mm; 7 ft) was developed from a special record-breaking Midget. In competition guise, it gave a better ride and, as a result, improved roadholding. In production form, there was enough space at the back for extra seats to be fitted. This new chassis was adopted for the D-type Midget production car introduced in 1931. The D-type (it acquired its name as a follow-on from the C-type production racing Midget) used the M-type's running gear. The M-type, with its 2057 mm (6 ft 9 in) wheelbase, continued in production as a two-seater, with the D-type offered with either open four-seater bodywork or a closed body rather like that of an M-type coupé.

The prototype competition machines made at that time were known by EX-for-experimental numbers, so it seemed quite natural to designate M.G.'s next model, which was introduced in late 1931, the F-type. And because it was a six-cylinder version of the D-type, it was called the Magna. The engine was not a new design, however, although M.G. tried to give the impression that it was. The 'new' 1271 cc power unit was basically that of a Wolseley Hornet with two extra cylinders added and a lot of sheet metal surrounding the cylinder block to disguise its origin. The F-type was given a wheelbase of 2388 mm (7 ft 10 in) to accommodate both the longer engine and the rear-seat passengers. It was also offered with bodywork like that of the D-type.

These new cars sold well alongside the evergreen M-type, as competition M.G.s went from success to success. However, they were underpowered, a fault that was made all too apparent by the extra weight brought about by their longer wheelbases and the extra passengers they could carry. This applied particularly to the Midget, which still had an engine of only 847 cc. Therefore Kimber started work immediately on a sensational new Midget with an engine uprated along racing lines and a body using all the competition styling, such as cutaway

RIGHT *M.G. lore before the war was very confusing. Normally, KN Magnettes, like this 1935 model, were built only as saloons. But some specialists, such as the London main dealers, University Motors, produced their own bodies, in this case a pretty 'Speed Model' tourer, on the saloon chassis – with, typically, an 'M.G.' registration number, obtained from the local licence office. Provided by Martin Warner.*

BELOW *Putting on the style. . . since the 1930s whenever people thought of a sports car, they thought of the shape first created for the M.G. J2. This 1933 model has been fitted, wisely, with the larger brakes of the J3 competition model. Provided by the Paradise Garage.*

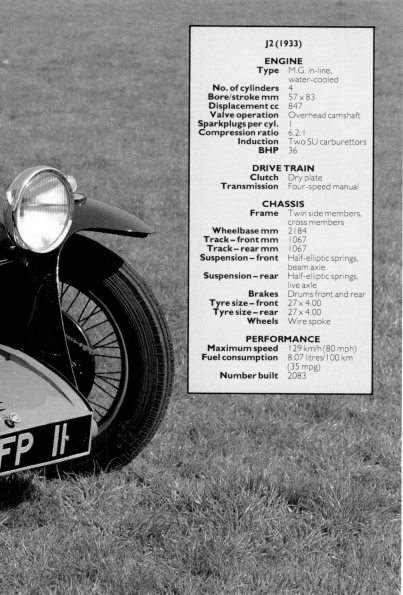

J2 (1933)	
ENGINE	
Type	M.G. in-line, water-cooled
No. of cylinders	4
Bore/stroke mm	57 × 83
Displacement cc	847
Valve operation	Overhead camshaft
Sparkplugs per cyl.	1
Compression ratio	6.2:1
Induction	Two SU carburettors
BHP	36
DRIVE TRAIN	
Clutch	Dry plate
Transmission	Four-speed manual
CHASSIS	
Frame	Twin side members, cross members
Wheelbase mm	2184
Track – front mm	1067
Track – rear mm	1067
Suspension – front	Half-elliptic springs, beam axle
Suspension – rear	Half-elliptic springs, live axle
Brakes	Drums front and rear
Tyre size – front	27 × 4.00
Tyre size – rear	27 × 4.00
Wheels	Wire spoke
PERFORMANCE	
Maximum speed	129 km/h (80 mph)
Fuel consumption	8.07 litres/100 km (35 mpg)
Number built	2083

doors, fold-flat windscreen, double-humped scuttle, cycle-type wings, and a large external slablike fuel tank at the back. This new Midget, called the J2 (what happened to the other letters of the alphabet is a mystery) was to set the style for sports cars for years and form the distinctive shape that took M.G. into the 1950s. Not only did the J2 look like a racing car, it felt like one when it was driven on the road. It had the fashionable stiff suspension of that era, and an engine that developed its maximum power (some 36 bhp) at no less than 5500 rpm, despite having only a two-bearing crankshaft. Its wheelbase of 2184 mm (7 ft 2 in) was the same as later versions of the D-type.

The J2 was introduced in August 1932, alongside a J1 open four-seat tourer on the same wheelbase. This latter car had the option of Salonette bodywork, but the J2 was the undoubted star, particularly as it cost little more than the M-type. Kimber was not slow to cash in on this success, fitting the J2's distinctive body to the Magna chassis, with a suitably lengthened bonnet, soon after the J2 had been introduced. The new Magna then adopted the F2 designation, and a four-seater Magna was designated the F3.

And just to keep the ball rolling, Kimber introduced in late 1932 yet another line – now that the 18/80 was on its last knockings – named the Magnette. This new six-cylinder car with a 1087 cc engine cost more than the Magna, but was intended at first as the basis of a new racing machine for the 1100 cc class. Nevertheless, these cars – called, logically, the K-types – were available with an even longer 2743 mm (9 ft) wheelbase, or a 2388 mm (7 ft 10in) base similar to that of the Magna. The track was increased to 1219 mm (4ft), halfway between the 18/80 Mark II (1321 mm; 4 ft 4 in) and the Midgets and Magnas (1067 mm; 3 ft 6 in) to provide more interior space for the open four-seater touring or pillarless four-door saloon bodywork on the long wheelbase chassis, and thus to justify the extra cost. An open two-seater sports body was offered on the shorter wheelbase chassis. In its original form, the Magnette's engine (the KA) was based closely on the Wolseley Hornet's, which had given rise to the Magna. As such, it did not produce much power. Therefore, soon after the long-wheelbase K1 and the short-wheelbase K2 had gone into production in February 1933, a more powerful KB engine became available. This improved engine was offered at first on the open cars, as they were more sporting in nature, with the earlier engine retained for the more sedate saloon. The Magnettes were usually fitted with the unsynchronized gearbox – called a 'crash' box by people who could not time their changes to perfection – in common with the other M.G. road cars, although a smoother racing-style, preselector gearbox could be ordered as an option.

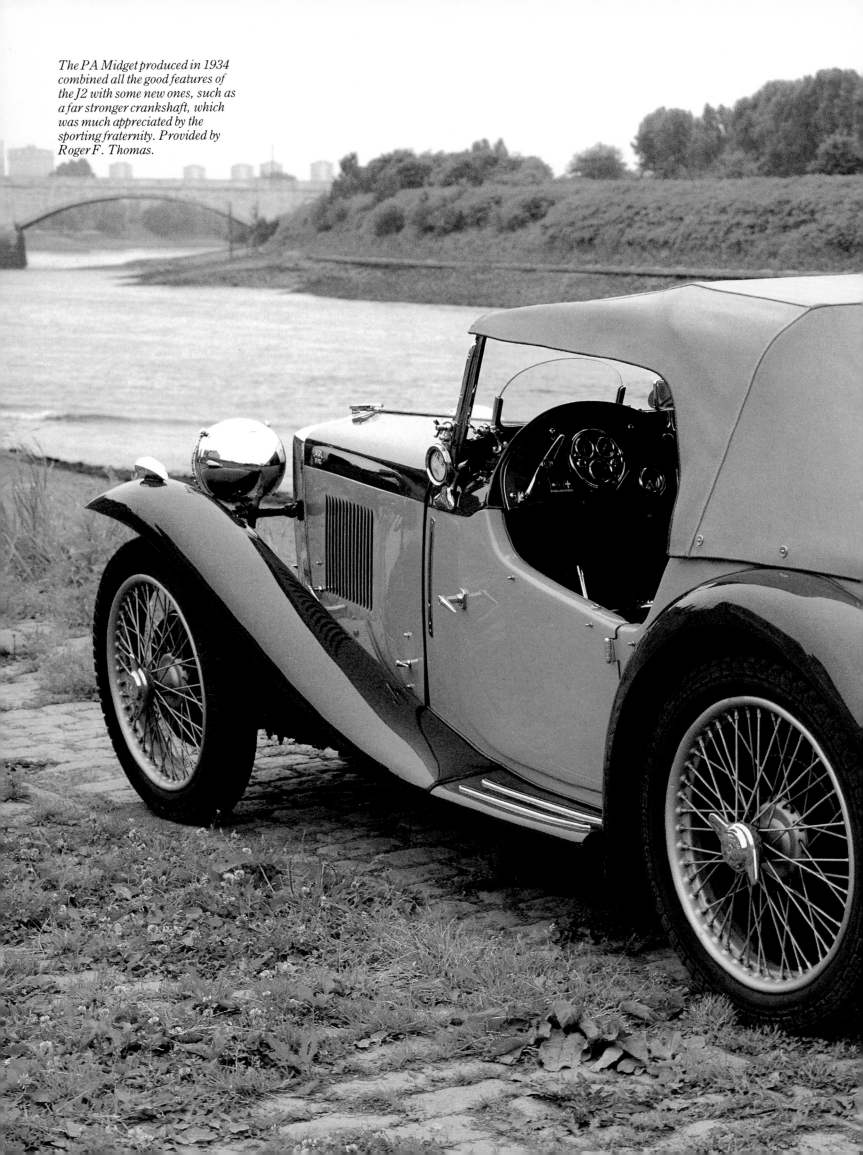

The PA Midget produced in 1934 combined all the good features of the J2 with some new ones, such as a far stronger crankshaft, which was much appreciated by the sporting fraternity. Provided by Roger F. Thomas.

RIGHT *Hardly any two L-type Magnas were exactly alike: normally they had swept wings like those on the K2, but quite frequently they were fitted with cycle-type wings for use in trials. Subsequently, many were rebuilt with later bodies, like this 1933 L1 model, which was fitted with an L2 cycle-wing body in 1944. It was a wonderful era for bespoke cars. Provided by Nicholas A. Dean.*

Magnette cost considerably more, however, so its power was stepped up to make it a genuine top-of-the-range model. The Magnette engine's stroke was lengthened to give it a capacity of 1271 cc; the new unit – with coil ignition – was called the KD. This was linked to the preselector gearbox which was made standard from June 1933.

With so much work going into development (and a huge effort into racing), it was hardly surprising that M.G.'s prices were creeping up: the expensive Magnettes, in particular, proved relatively hard to sell. The mainstay of the range continued to be the J2, despite its habit of breaking its two-bearing crankshaft, especially when driven by enthusiasts who considered revs to be an M.G.'s birthright. So the new Midget, the P-type, introduced in February 1934, had a sturdy new three-bearing 847 cc engine and a greater degree of standardization with the Magnette, which was to replace the Magna and was revised as the N-type.

The new Midget's wheelbase was increased slightly to 2210 mm (7 ft 3 in); the Magnette was standardized at 2440 mm (8 ft). The Midget retained its track of 1067 mm (3 ft 6 in), but the new Magnette used one of 1143 mm (3 ft 9 in), halfway between the Magna and the old Magnette. The N-type chassis, with its side members wider at the back than at the front, marked M.G.'s departure from the simple ladder-type

ABOVE *Kimber was very fond of fixed-head coupés, and one of the most attractive ever produced, the Airline – shown on a 1934 PA chassis – received a great deal of attention. Sadly, few were made by the specialist coachbuilder, H.W. Allingham, because a bigger standard car could be bought for the same price.*

LEFT *The NA Magnette, built in 1934 with new chassis and body, was one of the last models from the glorious period when technical development ran riot at Abingdon. Provided by B. Hague Sutton.*

Diversification

By this time, Kimber's creative genius was at its peak, for not only was M.G. making a bewildering array of competition cars, but the company's production cars were becoming even more varied: in March 1933, the Magna range went on to its L series with its existing 1067 mm (3 ft 6 in) track combined with the K2's 2388 mm (7 ft 10 in) wheelbase. The body variations were just as confusing because the L-type bore a distinct resemblance to the F2 and J2 in the centre of the body, and the K2 in its swept wings! This amazing juxtaposition, or cross-pollination, of parts to produce new models was typical of the ploys of contemporary car manufacturers, although, in the case of M.G., it contributed to a lowering of the profit margin, as hardly any two cars were exactly alike. They all needed individual attention at the production – and servicing – stages. Whenever a new feature was found to be helping to sell a model, where possible it was transferred to others.

The K2's elegant wings soon found their way on to the J2, although the range became a little simpler as the 18/80 Mark II was finally dropped, along with the open and closed four-seater Midget bodies. However, Kimber could not resist experimenting with closed bodies and he produced a Salonette-style Continental coupé on the L-type Magna chassis. The L-type also received more modern coil ignition in place of its earlier magneto, this engine now being called the KC. The

frame. The slab rear end was also abandoned on this car, the fuel tank being covered by a neat tail. Some left-over K2 bodies were fitted to the N-type chassis in addition to the normal open two- and four-seaters: this hybrid was known as the ND. In a similar way, surplus K1 pillarless saloon bodies were used on the N-type chassis to make up the KN. A pretty new Airline fixed-head coupé was offered on either Midget or Magnette chassis, and specialist coachbuilders, such as Allingham, Cresta and University Motors (who were also an M.G. main agent) produced their own bodies on M.G. chassis. So, although Kimber had made his range more viable, there was still a vast choice of cars, a feature that continues to endear M.G.s to the hearts of enthusiasts. The new P-type Midget was slightly more expensive than its predecessor, but it was much smoother and a little more roomy; the N-type cost marginally more than the Magna, but considerably less than the previous Magnette.

The P- and N-types sold extremely well, and M.G.'s fortunes were restored. Not in the racing world, however, as this expensive pastime was axed. Nevertheless, the fruits of competition were still filtering through, and the P-type's engine capacity was increased to 939 cc to give more power with a close-ratio gearbox, producing the PB for the 1936 model year. The N-type bodies were improved so that these later models became known as the NBs, before rationalization with the rest of Nuffield's products changed them dramatically.

Circuit Dust

Apart from Kimber's endeavours in the Land's End Trial, and a rather surprising victory by a 14/40 in a race at Buenos Aires, Argentina, in 1927, M.G. had virtually no competition history before 1929. M.G.s were sporty cars, but simply not suited to flat-out driving, mainly because of their primitive power units. But with the arrival of the overhead camshaft engines, everything changed. During the next five years, M.G.s achieved more than many manufacturers' products have done in a lifetime, so gripping the imagination of a generation that their exploits even formed the basis of such novels as *Circuit Dust* by Hollywood scriptwriter Barré Lyndon.

A man who might have stepped straight from the heroic tales of contemporary boys' magazines, Sir Francis Samuelson, drove an 18/80 single-handed to make the third best performance in the Monte Carlo Rally's Mont des Mules hill climb in 1929. Following this four Midgets and three 18/80s mopped up awards in the Land's End Trial that Easter. Three of these works Midgets then went on to win gold medals at Brooklands in June, followed by more successes.

It was obvious that M.G. now had competitive cars in both the large and small classes, so Kimber set about producing something really glamorous: a big sports car to match the Bentleys, which had just scored a hat-trick at Le Mans in 1929.

The 18/80's engine was reworked with a host of racing modifications, such as a new crankshaft, camshaft and pistons, cylinder head and dry-sump lubrication; the drive line was improved similarly. With the racing Bentleys for inspiration, the new M.G. became a veritable juggernaut. The Mark II's hefty chassis was retained largely unaltered,

With such a success behind them, the Midgets soon became popular cars in competition, winning races and hill climbs all over the world. Kimber was not content to rest on his laurels, however, spending a large part of the year planning a new model based on a short-lived French car called the Rally. The chassis of this 1100 cc competition car passed beneath the rear axle, giving it an exceptionally low centre of gravity. Charles devised a new rear spring mounting with pivots at the front end, leaving the rear free to slide in trunnions. The rigidity with which this system held the axle was one of the foundations of M.G.'s forthcoming reputation for exceedingly good roadholding. Charles's work on the valve timing had been passed on to production models, but engine develpment did not stop there. It was found that a great deal of extra power could be extracted from the Midget's engine, even in 750 cc form (to comply with the smallest class in international racing), by pursuing very high revs.

This was the engine that at first attracted record-breakers Captain George Eyston and Ernest Eldridge, although they promptly decided on the experimental chassis as well when they saw it at Abingdon. Clad in a suitably streamlined body, and fitted with modified Mark II brakes and a four-speed gearbox, this machine – called EX120 – captured several records from Austin at the Montlhéry track near Paris on 30 December 1930. It was then decided to supercharge EX120 in an attempt to become the first 750 cc car to exceed 160 km/h (100 mph) – a task made more imperative when Sir Malcolm Campbell raised the flying mile record to 151 km/h (94 mph) with an Austin Seven. After burning much midnight oil, the M.G. team returned to Montlhéry in

PRECEDING PAGES AND RIGHT *The last of the Montlhéry, or C-type, Midgets was number 44, built in 1932. It came complete with an optional supercharger, which can be seen mounted alongside its SU carburettor between the dumb irons at the front of the chassis. Provided by Allan Bentley.*

LEFT *How did the giant Eyston prise himself free from the high sides of his burning Midget? From left to right: Works manager George Propert, George Eyston, racing mechanic Reg Jackson, Cecil Kimber and Jimmy Palmes survey the wreck with one side torn off, back at Abingdon in 1931.*

although it received a competition body with cycle-type wings and four seats to meet contemporary international sports car racing regulations. This was the 18/100 road-racing model, a Mark III that became known as the Tiger or Tigress, depending on which sex you considered the more formidable. Despite its dry-sump lubrication system, the overweight Tiger lasted only a couple of hours of the Brooklands Double Twelve race in 1930 before retiring with bearing trouble. Intensive development followed, but this expensive car – it cost nearly twice as much as a basic 18/80 – showed a marked dislike for sustained high speed, and only five were built.

It was a disappointing start to M.G.'s first serious racing season – but the Midgets were to save Abingdon's honour. No fewer than six were entered for the Brooklands race that was graced so briefly by the Mark III. Hubert Charles had carried out some work on their rather conservative valve timing, boosting the power by a third to 27 bhp. These cars were fitted with special Brooklands exhaust systems, cutaway doors to allow the occupants to lean out to counter the effects of centrifugal force during hectic cornering, and fold-flat screens for minimum wind resistance. They ran beautifully throughout the long race to win the team prize from the rival Austin Sevens, which had enjoyed far more development. The main inspiration behind these cars were two market gardeners, William Edmondson and Cecil Randall. Therefore – in the manner of those times – the team was given a nickname: The Tomato Growers!

February the following year to achieve that object, breaking four records, including the one for five kilometres – at 165.97 km/h (103.13 mph).

Glory at Brooklands

This was a startling achievement that shook the world, particularly Britain, and did wonders for M.G.'s reputation. It also encouraged Kimber to launch a new 750 cc racing model, the Montlhéry Midget, or C-type, with or without a supercharger. However, the highly specialized record-breaking engine needed complete revision by Charles before it could go into production, which was achieved by shortening the stroke – an ideal recipe for high revs! Frantic efforts by the entire Abingdon workforce saw 14 of the new Midgets at Brooklands for the Double Twelve race in 1931, facing almost as many Austin Sevens and Riley Nines. Abingdon's preparations had been exceptionally thorough, with every driver and member of the pit crew receiving an intense briefing on what he had to do and the exact speed to be averaged.

Practically every member of the M.G. staff was on hand to see the results of their labour: the first five places in the race went to the Midgets (with the Earl of March and Chris Staniland winning), plus the coveted team prize. It was heralded as one of the greatest triumphs by a single make in the history of motor racing – made all the more extraordinary by the fact that it was the model's début. More was to

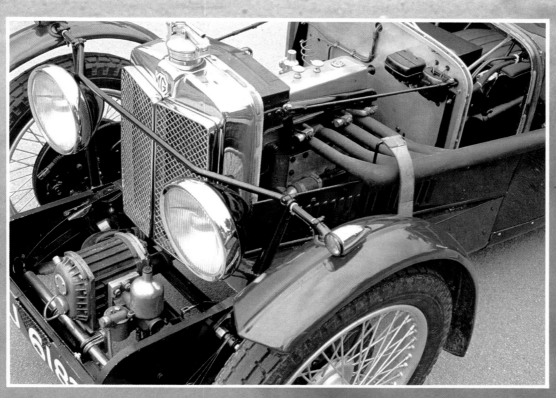

18/100 Six Mark III (1930)

ENGINE

Type	M.G. in-line, water-cooled
No. of cylinders	6
Bore/stroke mm	69 × 110
Displacement cc	2468
Valve operation	Overhead camshaft
Sparkplugs per cyl.	2
Compression ratio	Approx 8:1
Induction	Two SU carburettors
BHP	83 to 96 according to tune

DRIVE TRAIN

Clutch	Wet cork
Transmission	Four-speed manual

CHASSIS

Frame	Twin side members, cross members
Wheelbase mm	2896
Track – front mm	1320
Track – rear mm	1320
Suspension – front	Half-elliptic springs, beam axle
Suspension – rear	Half-elliptic springs, live axle
Brakes	Drums front and rear
Tyre size	29 × 5.00
Wheels	Wire spoke

PERFORMANCE

Maximum speed	Approx 145 km/h (90 mph) to 161 km/h (100 mph) according to tune
Fuel consumption	14.12 litres/100 km (20 mpg)
Number built	5

The 18/100 Mark III built by M.G. in 1930 was one of the most spectacular models in appearance and specification – but suffered from a lack of development and a high price. Provided by C. Barker.

JB 855

come that year, however, as Montlhéry Midget driver Norman Black won both the Irish Grand Prix and the Tourist Trophy in Ulster – which, with the Double Twelve, made up the three most important races in the United Kingdom in 1931.

Once the racing season was over, record-breaking activities resumed, with Eyston determined to crack the 100 for an hour. Fitted with a rebuilt engine and tidied-up bodywork, the gallant Midget smashed the record at 162.7 km/h (101.1 mph) before being involved in one of the most dramatic moments in M.G.'s sporting history. Apparently the engine ran a bearing, setting fire to the sump oil. As the giant Eyston passed out of sight of the M.G. crew, he wriggled free from the high-sided streamlined cockpit, and jumped out as the car slowed to 97 km/h (60 mph).

Using a technique perfected in fox hunting, he avoided serious injury, and the blazing car ran into a sandbank. At that moment, the driver of another car under test on the track pulled up and rushed him to hospital. By the time the M.G. men had reached the scene, flames were enveloping the car. They clawed frantically at the cockpit, only to find there was no one inside – or indeed anywhere else! As Thornley said in his classic account of M.G.'s racing and record-breaking days, *Maintaining the Breed:* 'It is not hard to imagine the tremendous cavalcade of emotions which flowed through these men in this brief dramatic episode which marked the end of the useful life of EX120.'

Once they learned that Eyston was not too seriously injured, they were happy: they had already built a successor to EX120, called EX127 after its design office number. This Midget was built to the minimum section that could enclose Eyston, with its transmission line offset to pass beside him, rather than under him. Eyston's partner, the engineer Eldridge, took EX127 up to 177.48 km/h (110.28 mph) at Montlhéry despite his poor eyesight, before Eyston himself, clad in special asbestos overalls, achieved 184.70 km/h (114.77 mph) at the same track on the way to 190.53 km/h (118.39 mph) at Pendine Sands in Carmarthen Bay, South Wales, in February 1932. They knew they could reach Kimber's requirement of 190 km/h (120 mph) – it was just a matter of time – although they had to resort to all manner of dodges, such as shielding bolt heads with Plasticine to reduce wind resistance!

EX127, which by now had become known as the Magic Midget, also proved its versatility in the racing season by beating most of the opposition in what was then the world's fastest race, the Junior Car Club's 500-mile event at Brooklands. Its engine blew up in the race (won by Ronnie Horton's single-seater supercharged C-type), when Eyston's co-driver and mechanic, Bert Denly, eased off suddenly to avoid a fatal crash that had occurred in front of him.

Eddie Hall took the standing-start mile and kilometre class records with a supercharged C-type in November 1932, before the Magic Midget returned to Montlhéry to capture the rest of the records up to 12 hours – and, almost incidentally, achieve Kimber's much-desired 190 km/h (120 mph)! Then a team, including Eyston, Denly and Hall, used a J3 Midget to take further records up to 24 hours.

The J3 Midget, officially a road vehicle, was a supercharged version of the J2. An out-and-out racing example of this car, the J4, was introduced at the same time in 1932. It had Magnette-style steering and the larger Magna brakes to cope with its increased performance. It was a typical example of M.G.'s policy at the time of making road-going cars that could be used in club racing and pure racing cars at reasonable prices.

M.G.'s competition successes were rewarding, not only for morale at Abingdon, but also in the form of record sales that year while many other small manufacturers were going under. The racing cars cost far more to make than they were sold for but, as accountants such as Thornley pointed out, the publicity they gained was invaluable. It is also doubtful if M.G. could have produced such an array of attractive new machines had it not been for the enforced development of racing.

The greatest M.G.

One of the most successful products of this policy was the K3 Magnette introduced late in 1932. This was basically a supercharged K2 and was to become M.G.'s most famous racing car. Its preselector gearbox was ideal for racing in that it left the driver's hands free for the wild swinging movements so necessary in those days of whippy chassis, rough roads and skinny tyres. With this system, a predetermined gear ratio was selected with a lever before it was needed – for instance in a corner – and then engaged by a foot pedal at the appropriate moment.

RIGHT AND BELOW *The K3 Magnette became one of the most famous M.G.s ever made. It won numerous events, including Britain's oldest road race, the Tourist Trophy, and the 1100 cc class in the Italian classic, the Mille Miglia, in 1933. Thirty-three of these cars were built between 1932 and 1934, including prototypes. Most of them had the traditional, J2-inspired bodywork of the type fitted to Briggs Cunningham's 1933 example on the right. But others, such as Dudley Gahagan's 1934 model, shown below in an M.G. Car Club historic event at Silverstone in 1982, and the record-breaker, EX135, were subsequently equipped with more aerodynamic coachwork.*

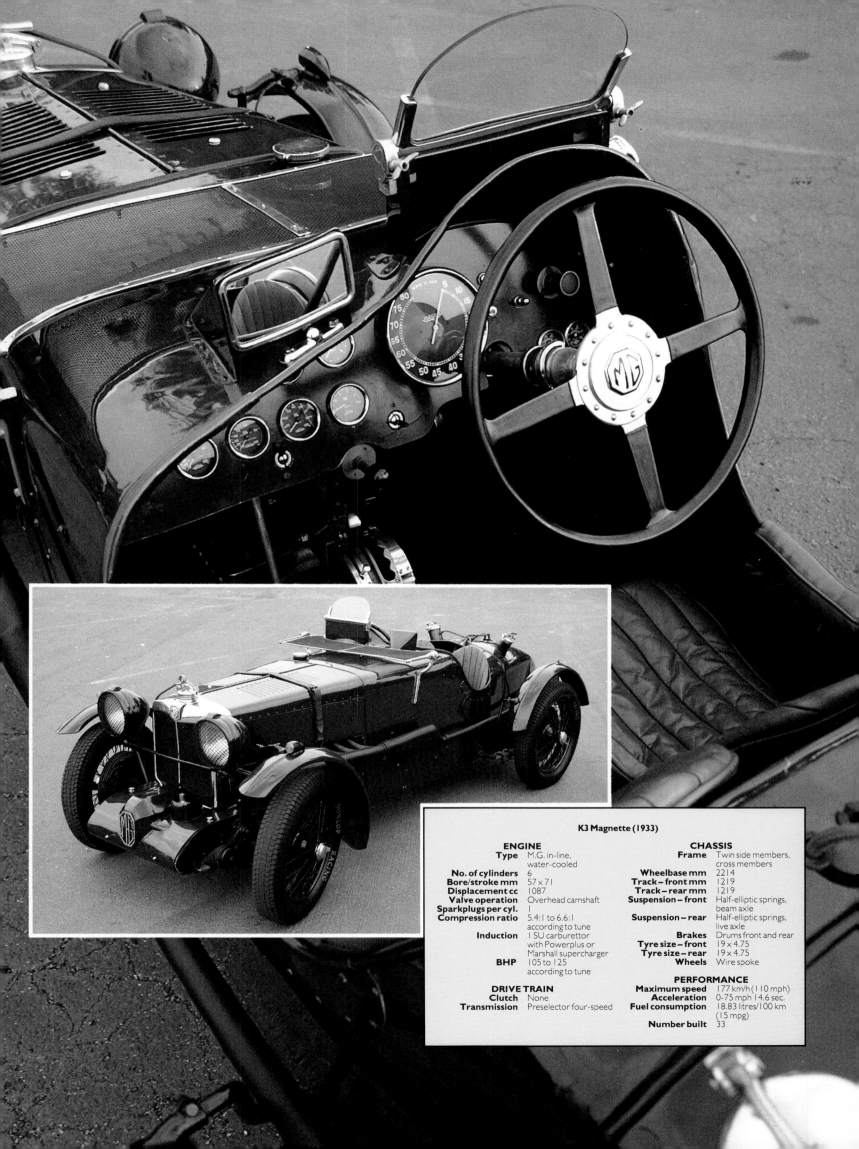

K3 Magnette (1933)

ENGINE		CHASSIS	
Type	M.G. in-line, water-cooled	**Frame**	Twin side members, cross members
No. of cylinders	6	**Wheelbase mm**	2214
Bore/stroke mm	57 × 71	**Track – front mm**	1219
Displacement cc	1087	**Track – rear mm**	1219
Valve operation	Overhead camshaft	**Suspension – front**	Half-elliptic springs, beam axle
Sparkplugs per cyl.	1		
Compression ratio	5.4:1 to 6.6:1 according to tune	**Suspension – rear**	Half-elliptic springs, live axle
Induction	1 SU carburettor with Powerplus or Marshall supercharger	**Brakes**	Drums front and rear
		Tyre size – front	19 × 4.75
		Tyre size – rear	19 × 4.75
BHP	105 to 125 according to tune	**Wheels**	Wire spoke
		PERFORMANCE	
DRIVE TRAIN		**Maximum speed**	177 km/h (110 mph)
Clutch	None	**Acceleration**	0-75 mph 14.6 sec.
Transmission	Preselector four-speed	**Fuel consumption**	18.83 litres/100 km (15 mpg)
		Number built	33

LEFT AND ABOVE *This open 1934 NA, shown with its supercharged engine, is an ex-works car driven in the 1935 Monte Carlo Rally by Humfrey Symons and Abingdon mechanic Freddie Kindell. They suffered appalling conditions before crashing while vying for the lead! But the car survived to be enjoyed today by Mike Allison.*

The K3 was intended for road racing but, nevertheless, a prototype competed in the Monte Carlo Rally in 1933, storming up the Mont des Mules to set an 1100 cc record.

Greater exploits were to come. Three K3s were entered for the classic round-Italy road race, the Mille Miglia, in 1933. Former 'Bentley Boy' Sir Henry Birkin, with Bernard Rubin, thrashed the rival Maseratis before he had valve trouble in his K3, leaving Eyston and Count Giovanni Lurani to win their class. Earl Howe, and University Motors salesman Hugh Hamilton – who was to achieve even greater things in a J4 – backed them up with second in class. No other marque had three cars running at the finish, so the team award went to the two M. G. s – the first time it had been won by a non-Italian make in the history of the Mille Miglia. Such was the importance of this victory that two future Kings of England, Edward, Prince of Wales, and Prince George, attended a celebration dinner in London.

M. G. victories came thick and fast after that. In 1933 Hamilton ran away from the 800 cc field in Germany's Eifelrennen at the Nürburgring with his J4. Then, shortly afterwards, the greatest driver of the time,

the Italian Tazio Nuvolari, agreed to race a K3 in the Tourist Trophy. He broke the 1100 cc class lap record seven times before winning the event – which was based on a handicap like many contemporary classics – by 40 seconds from Hamilton's J4. In fact, Hamilton came near to beating him, losing time only by playing safe and refuelling while Nuvolari was left with a nearly dry tank at the end. The Italian's average of 126.57 km/h (78.65 mph) remained the fastest winning speed in the TT for 18 years.

Then Hall mopped up the Brooklands 500 with a single-seater K3 before the Magic Midget, fitted with Hamilton's TT engine, and a new, even smaller body, returned to Montlhéry in late 1933 for slim-line Denly to raise the flying mile record to 207.01 km/h (128.63 mph). Eyston was too big to squeeze into the new body, which was designed to reduce wind resistance.

The racing Midgets and Magnettes continued to win all manner of events for years to come, but even more intriguing M. G. s were on the way. Horton had a single-seater body made for a K3 along the lines of his C-type, and Eyston had a Magic Magnette constructed with offset transmission and two bodies: one for road racing and one for the track and record-breaking. This K3 was called EX135 and was known as the Humbug, because of its distinctive brown-and-cream striped colour scheme, like the popular British confectionery. With this car he took 12 records – including 194.54 km (120.88 miles) in the hour – from Horton at Montlhéry in 1934.

Production of the J4 had ended late in 1933 after only nine cars had been built because soaring power outputs were making the engine too fast for its tiny chassis. The Magnette's frame was too big, however, so the best features of the new P- and N-types were combined to produce the Q-type Midget for the 1934 season. Fitted with a K3-style body and a new Zoller supercharger, this proved to be a formidable competition machine. However, the science of supercharging was moving at such a rate – and cost – that forced induction was outlawed for the Tourist Trophy in 1934. So, for the Ulster classic, Abingdon extracted more power from an unblown N-type engine and fitted it to a Magnette chassis equipped with special racing bodywork, naming the resultant model the NE. The formula was successful, but only just, as an NE gave M.G. a hat-trick in the TT by just 17 seconds.

It was at this time that reliability trials (in which supposedly standard cars had to cover a testing terrain, including fearsome and muddy hills) were becoming very popular with the sporting fraternity. The J2 Midget, with its ultra-light bodywork and willing engine, became one of the most attractive cars in these events, so Abingdon decided to weigh in with a works team to publicize the new P-type. Three of these cars, driven by Maurice Toulmin, Jack Bastock and Mac Macdermid, and called the Cream Crackers because of their inevitable brown and cream colours, were outstandingly successful.

Back on the track the Q-type was going the same way as its predecessor, with engine development making it too fast for its leaf-sprung chassis. Charles, therefore, ever willing to develop new ideas, designed a backbone chassis with torsion bar independent suspension all round: an incredibly advanced machine for its day. Using the latest line in Q-type engines, and equipped with a genuine single-seater body, it needed little imagination to see that the M.G. company was on its way towards building a grand prix car! Despite an apparent lack of development, this car was reasonably successful until the inevitable happened.

RIGHT *As rallying is one of Britain's biggest spectator sports today, so were reliability trials in the 1930s. Car manufacturers were not supposed to enter teams – so that private competitors had a fair chance – but the events were so prestigious that M.G. backed three top drivers to the hilt in 1934, providing them with PA Midgets painted in the works colours of brown and cream. They soon became known as the Cream Crackers as a result and scored many successes in a highly competitive field. Car provided by Bob Williams.*

LEFT *Supercharging reached new levels when Hubert Charles collaborated in the design of a new Zoller system, with the result that by 1936 the 750 cc engine of the Q-type Midget was giving more power in relation to its size than any other unit. But the 100-146 bhp produced by these engines was too much for their leaf-sprung chassis, so the R-type with independent suspension was developed for 1935. This Q-type replica is shown competing at the Prescott hill climb in 1975.*

Still-born M.G.s

M.G. sales had fallen to around half those of the 2500 produced in the peak year, 1932, and the company was making a loss. The main reason for the decline was the rising price of the cars, supplemented by increasing insurance premiums that accompanied their high-performance image. It was also a time of great upheaval for the newly formed Nuffield Organization, set up to rationalize William Morris's myriad empire, including M.G. Morris's new managing director, a ruthless production engineering expert named Leonard Lord, began welding the group together and disposing of parts that did not quite fit in – such as the M.G. design office. The first victim of this streamlining process was M.G.'s racing programme; to the horror of all the staff at Abingdon, and enthusiasts everywhere, it was axed in the middle of the 1935 season. The M.G. and Wolseley concerns were transferred from their previously favoured position under William Morris's aegis to Nuffield corporate ownership. Lord decided that this

meant the Wolseley-based overhead cam engines had to go, and would be replaced with the far cheaper Morris pushrod units. New projects, such as a V8 sports car and an improved R-type, were cancelled. Charles was transferred to the Morris head office at Cowley, under Vic Oak, and future M.Gs were visualized by Lord simply as superior versions of Morris and Wolseley products.

There was little anybody, even Kimber, could do about it: jobs were at a premium in those days, especially out at Abingdon, away from the big urban centres. But Lord could not crush the octagon as easily as that. The Cream Crackers cost little to run and they had been reinforced by a team of NE Magnettes called the Three Musketeers. They continued to dominate trials, as private owners raced on with their Midgets, Magnettes and record-breakers. However, the new M.G.s would be very different machines, although thanks to the spirit of Abingdon they remained individual sports cars while selling in far larger numbers.

Hard reality

The revolution that swept through Abingdon in the summer of 1935 involved not only the end of the works racing cars, but also the amalgamation of M.G. with the Morris and Wolseley concerns at Cowley. This took place in July 1935 as the projected V8 sports car was cancelled and Hubert Charles was transferred to Cowley. Kimber remained at Abingdon for much of the time, although there was little that he could do without the approval of Leonard Lord.

To begin with, Lord said he did not want any more M.G. sports cars. They were more trouble than they were worth to his plans for streamlining the Nuffield Organization. But Kimber still had a lot of influence and rallied enough support to change Lord's mind. The results of Lord's initial edict and Kimber's fight to keep M.G. as a separate marque were seen in the new cars introduced in 1936.

The car that Lord favoured was announced first, in October 1935. This was the M.G. Two-Litre, based closely on Wolseley's Super Six. It was far bigger than anything M.G. had produced before – bigger even than the ill-fated Tigress – and aimed at the market for luxury sports saloons. Although Lord thought that all he had to do to sell a Wolseley at an inflated price was to put an M.G. radiator on it, Kimber's lobby persuaded him otherwise. 'Mister M.G.', as Kimber was known, was allowed to design a new body. To his credit, he did a very good job, making the new S-series M.G. an exceptionally attractive machine. With its 3124 mm (10 ft 3 in) wheelbase and 1356 mm (4 ft 5 in) track, and price of £375, it offered excellent value for money compared with its immediate predecessor, the KN Magnette, which had cost £399.

Everything except the body was relatively run-of-the-mill: it had an ordinary swept-up chassis, rather than M.G.'s established underslung one, and a pushrod engine instead of the glorious overhead cam; but it cruised comfortably at 129 km/h (80 mph), although it took rather a long time to reach this speed. The Two-Litre, or SA as it was known, was a heavy car and benefited from the use of hydraulic brakes, which Kimber, in a rather blinkered attitude, had refused to fit to previous M.G.s, maintaining that the old-style cable brakes were more dependable. Sadly, the SA suffered from the very inefficiency within the Nuffield Organization that Lord was trying to eradicate. Far too many people were involved in decisions affecting the cars with the result that models were often delayed. The SA went through numerous detail changes in order to use the standardized components supplied by

PRECEDING PAGES *Cecil Kimber did an excellent job in designing the bodywork for a completely new range of M.G.s demanded of Abingdon. Although the VA was much larger than its predecessors, it retained their characteristic charm, as Frances Adam's 1937 tourer demonstrates.*

Wolseley, who was also evolving new models at that time.

However, the biggest blow to M.G. was the introduction at this time of a brilliant rival, the S.S. Jaguar, a sporting saloon with a powerful new 2½-litre engine. This car was produced by a specialist independent manufacturer that M.G. had completely underestimated. The previous S.S. cars had been of a rather flashy nature that was not backed up by a glorious competition record like M.G. But the S.S. Jaguar was designed by the proprietor William Lyons, a stylist at least the equal of Kimber. He also ran his firm in a thoroughly autocratic manner, which meant that the S.S. Jaguar went straight into production, whereas it took until the spring of 1936 for the floundering Nuffield Organization to provide enough parts and decide on the production specification for the SA.

This process was not helped by increasing the capacity of the engine from the prototype's 2062 cc to 2288 cc in an attempt to put it on a par with the Jaguar's 2663 cc unit. This sort of alteration could be done in a matter of days when M.G. was independent, but it took months when it became yet another relatively unimportant job for Morris Engines. In the meantime, hundreds of disillusioned customers switched their orders from the M.G., which was not ready, to the S.S. Jaguar, which certainly was.

Kimber used this situation to keep up the pressure for a new sports car to replace the PB, now that its overhead cam engine was being phased out. The SA might have been left at the market place, but M.G. could accept this set-back as the car was a new venture. However, the company certainly could not afford a repetition of this if it meant being forced to produce a rebodied Morris or Wolseley instead of sports cars, the line that had made its reputation. So Lord and Kimber compromised: Kimber, with the help of Charles, could produce a new two-seater sports car (the tiny four-seaters were rightly considered to have been outmoded) if he stuck closely to Morris or Wolseley components and made it a universal sports car, to replace both the Midget and the Magnette. Lord said this course of action would bring a reasonable profit, rather than wasting a lot of money developing two lines that would compete with each other.

A new Midget

So Kimber and Charles went away and designed a brand-new Midget, as that was M.G.'s best-selling line. In reality, they had two engines to choose from: a small one used in the Morris Eight, and a larger 1292 cc four-cylinder unit fitted in the Morris Ten. Because these were pushrod engines, they were not as efficient as the P-type's overhead cam unit, so they chose the larger one, which, ironically, had been developed from the original Bullnose engine!

It was back to basics for the new Midget (designated the T-series) introduced at the London Motor Show in 1936, with no choice of transmission other than the existing Morris/Wolseley units. But Charles was allowed to design a new chassis – using the Q-type for inspiration – with a 2388 mm (7 ft 10 in) wheelbase, and a 1143 mm (3 ft 9 in) track. This made it much bigger than the PB, more of a Magnette, in fact: therefore, with Kimber's far roomier body, it did effectively replace both models. Its suspension was softer, in keeping with saloon car trends; it had the new hydraulic brakes; and it weighed 45 kg (100 lb) more – but it was 90 kg (200 lb) lighter than the ND, and the engine produced 50 bhp in tuned form, so it was just as fast as the old Midget and Magnette.

The new engine also had much more torque than the PB's smaller unit, and the new car was considerably easier to drive. M.G. enthusiasts were dismayed at first by the wholesale changes, but their loyalty to the marque outweighed their memories of the ear-splitting, kidney-shaking PB. Therefore they tried the new Midget: to their amazement they found that this 'soft and silent' new car went as well as it looked, and they liked it. This was the start of the immortal T-series that was to blaze an export trail for M.G., particularly in the United

LEFT *The 1937 TA illustrated was the first of a new range of M.G. Midgets that was to make Abingdon one of the world's foremost sports car producers. Provided by Alastair Naylor, owned by Keith Storey.*

BELOW *The WA with three-position drophead coupé bodywork by Tickford was the largest and most luxurious M.G. of its day. This car bears the chassis number 0251, indicating that it is the first of its line. Why 0251, rather than number 1? In fact, Abingdon 251 was the factory's telephone number! Provided by Nigel Hough.*

States, and take Abingdon to the threshold of mass production.

The process of assuring enthusiasts that the TA, as the new Midget was called, was a first-class car was helped when Kimber persuaded Lord Nuffield that the publicity gained by the Cream Crackers and the Three Musketeers trials teams was worth more than the cost of providing them with six new cars and paying their expenses. He could not go too far, however, as Nuffield was still firmly set against spending large sums on competition, as he had made clear through Lord, his able lieutenant. Consequently, the TAs used by these teams to dominate the 1937 trials season were little modified, apart from being fitted with aluminium bodies and cycle-type wings; their engines were only slightly tuned and the gearboxes on these cars were equipped with the lower Wolseley saloon car ratios.

Renowned S.S. Jaguar driver Tommy Wisdom was also given a Two-Litre saloon to drive in the 1937 Mille Miglia, but he found that its great bulk was rather unwieldy and he crashed on a wet road. Other racing efforts, although carried out with clandestine works support, were more successful. M.G.s – particularly a team of R-types entered by London's Bellevue Garage – won numerous events on road and track. Two of the most successful private entrants were the German Bobby Kohlrausch, who bought the Magic Midget and used it to great effect in Continental hill climbs, and Major A.T.G. 'Goldie' Gardner, who took over Ronnie Horton's old single-seater K3. He set the Brooklands Outer Circuit 1100 cc record at 200.2 km/h (124.4 mph) in August 1936, before Kohlrausch took the Midget up to 226.3 km/h (140.6 mph) for the flying mile at Frankfurt in October that year. This amazing speed for a 750 cc car was achieved with the help of a German-made bronze cylinder head fitted to an Abingdon-tuned supercharged Q-type engine. The reason for this curious arrangement was that Abingdon could not have won approval for developing such a

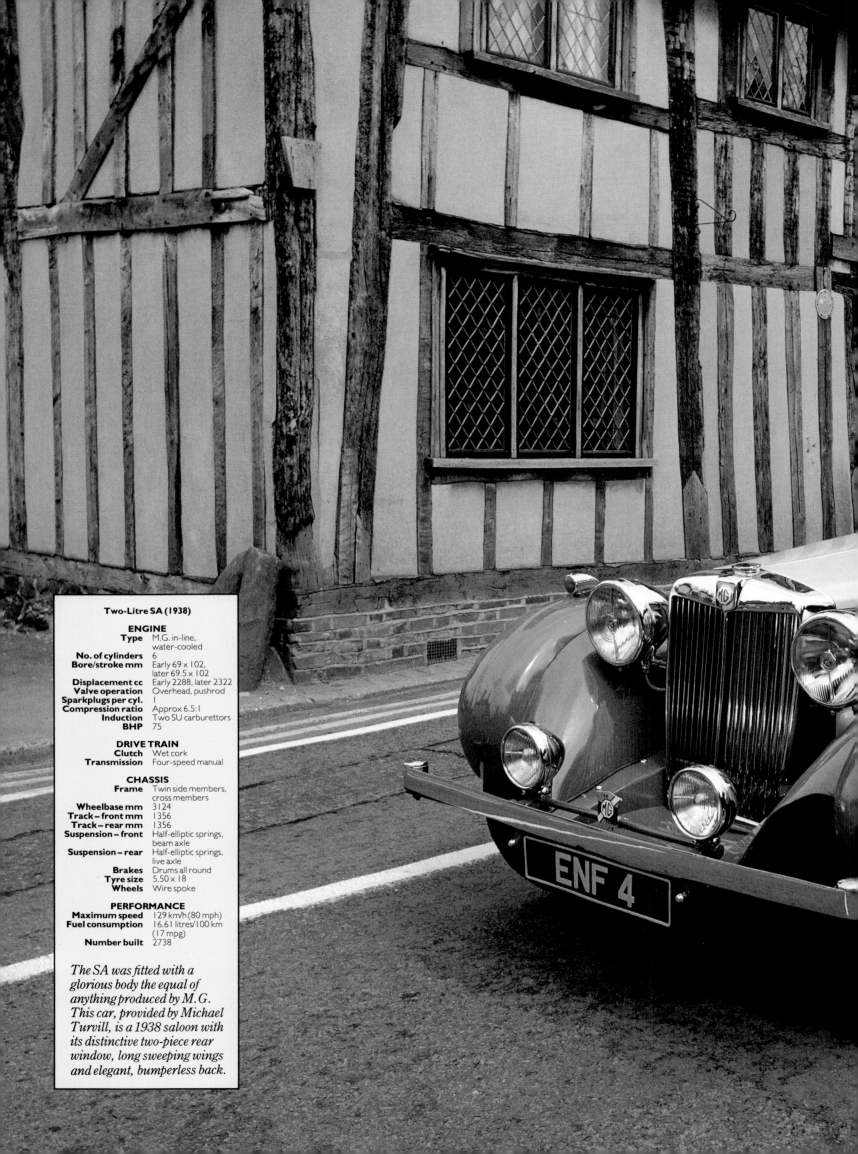

Two-Litre SA (1938)

ENGINE

Type	M.G. in-line, water-cooled
No. of cylinders	6
Bore/stroke mm	Early 69 × 102, later 69.5 × 102
Displacement cc	Early 2288, later 2322
Valve operation	Overhead, pushrod
Sparkplugs per cyl.	1
Compression ratio	Approx 6.5:1
Induction	Two SU carburettors
BHP	75

DRIVE TRAIN

Clutch	Wet cork
Transmission	Four-speed manual

CHASSIS

Frame	Twin side members, cross members
Wheelbase mm	3124
Track – front mm	1356
Track – rear mm	1356
Suspension – front	Half-elliptic springs, beam axle
Suspension – rear	Half-elliptic springs, live axle
Brakes	Drums all round
Tyre size	5.50 × 18
Wheels	Wire spoke

PERFORMANCE

Maximum speed	129 km/h (80 mph)
Fuel consumption	16.61 litres/100 km (17 mpg)
Number built	2738

The SA was fitted with a glorious body the equal of anything produced by M.G. This car, provided by Michael Turvill, is a 1938 saloon with its distinctive two-piece rear window, long sweeping wings and elegant, bumperless back.

cylinder head, but the tuning could be put down to simple servicing!

Naturally, Gardner had to have a bronze head after that and he had one made by Brooklands tuning ace Robin Jackson along the same lines for his six-cylinder engine. It was then fitted to the unit prepared by Reg Jackson – no relation – at Abingdon, again as part of normal servicing! As a result, Gardner took the flying kilometre record at 238.5 km/h (148.8 mph) with the K3 in October 1937 on the same stretch of autobahn that Kohlrausch had used.

Meanwhile, the Nuffield men were occupied on completely different lines. They were anxious to propagate their new family of M.G.s with a larger and a smaller version of the SA. The smaller car, the VA, came first, halfway through 1937. It was based on the contemporary Wolseley Twelve, with a 1548 cc four-cylinder engine, a wheelbase of 2743 mm (9 ft) and a track of 1270 mm (4 ft 2 in). It was offered with similar four-seater body styles to those of the SA, in open tourer, saloon or drophead coupé forms. It took just as long to put into production as the SA, and it was not until the summer of 1938 that the larger WA made its appearance. This was almost exactly like the SA, except that it had a wider rear track of 1448 mm (4 ft 9 in) to take even more luxurious coachwork and a larger six-cylinder engine, of 2561 cc, to haul along the extra weight. These three cars, the SA, VA and WA, offered a similar performance with leisurely acceleration, but a maximum speed of more than 130 km/h (80 mph), which could be held in relative comfort. When viewed as luxurious tourers, rather than nimble, hell-for-leather sports cars, they were good machines, offering the same excellent value for money as S.S. Jaguars. They also helped take M.G.'s sales to nearly 3000 in 1938, which was even more than the boom time in 1932 and double that of 1935.

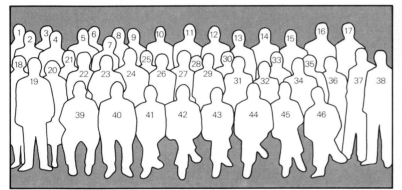

ABOVE *From their earliest days, the Abingdon workforce gained a reputation for skill, endeavour and never a strike. Here are some of the senior men and women pictured just before World War 2.*

1 Ralph Hewson
2 Victor Vines
3 Syd Haddock
4 Jock Craigmile
5 Harold Robinson
6 Horace Clewley
7 Jack Reed
8 Bill Smith
9 Syd Enever
10 Percy Watson

11 Hector Cox
12 Denby Jones
13 Syd Good
14 Percy Hughes
15 Bill Higgs
16 Jack Lewis
17 Reg Howes
18 Miss Pauline
19 John Pennock
20 Grace Lewis

21 Reg Jackson
22 Charles Martin
23 George Denton
24 John Bull
25 George King
26 Gordon Phillips
27 Marjorie Prickett
28 Frank Stevens
29 Miss Calcutt
30 Jack Lowndes

31 Madge Wakelin
32 Morag McLennan
33 Harry Rummins
34 Sam Nash
35 Harry Herring
36 Les Shurrock
37 George Morris
38 Percy Kent
39 Cecil Cousins
40 Mr Lepine

41 Dick Maynard
42 George Propert
43 Cecil Kimber
44 Bill Slingsby
45 John Thornley
46 George Tuck

With the lower-drag bodywork and additional power, EX135's driver, Gardner, covered the flying mile at 301.94 km/h (187.62 mph) on the Frankfurt autobahn in November 1938. It was a huge improvement on the old record – by nearly 65 km/h (40 mph) – but it was achieved with ease. In any case, Gardner liked to break records in a conservative manner, so that he could go back again later for a double dose of thrills and publicity! Needless to say he returned to Germany – only four months before war broke out – and raised the record to 327.5 km/h (203.5 mph) on another autobahn at Dessau. It was just the sort of inspiration that Britain needed with war clouds gathering; the news was received in May 1939 in a manner at least as ecstatic as when M.G. first cleared 160 km/h (100 mph) with a 750 cc car in 1931.

Naturally, the Cream Crackers and Musketeers benefited from the slight easing of budgets at Abingdon in the 1938 season. Mounting opposition from works Austins and Singers, plus purpose-built cars such as Allards with large American V8 engines, meant that they had to seek more power. As a result, six new cars were built, three for the Cream Crackers and three for the Musketeers, and a third team was formed, the Blue Bustards, to operate in Scotland. They received two of the previous year's Cream Crackers, plus a third TA that had been driven by Goff Imhof, who had tied with Cream Cracker leader Maurice Toulmin in the 1936 Experts' Trial.

The 1938 Cream Crackers – still resplendent in their brown and cream colour scheme – had VA engines, which were soon bored out to take WA pistons, raising the capacity to 1708 cc. The red-painted Musketeers (the Bustards were in Scottish blue) pursued a different line with supercharged TA engines. The two leading teams once again enjoyed a great deal of success; the Cream Crackers were marginally more successful, winning the national team championship. By then, trials were in decline as a major sporting attraction, with war on the way and increasing specialization taking much of the enjoyment out of them for the average participant.

It was in August 1938, however, that the TA range was extended to include a drophead coupé. This was a two-seater that fitted in well with the larger S, V and W ranges because it was built by the same specialist firm, Tickford, that was responsible for the other dropheads. It was also especially significant in that it was 102 mm (4 in) wider across the seats, making it feel much roomier inside. Naturally, it cost more, but it was considerably more comfortable, although the extra weight reduced its performance a little.

The performance, however, was soon to be improved, in April 1939, by fitting a better engine – a modified version of the new Morris Ten

ABOVE *Racing in England before the war was confined to Brooklands, Donington and Crystal Palace – so club folk found their enjoyment in trials, frequently over the most tortuous farm tracks. This classic picture of a TA well illustrates the ordeals they survived in the name of competition.*

RIGHT *Numerous circuits stage a bewildering array of races in Britain today – with few classes more popular than those for M.G. T-types. Glyn Giusti is shown at Silverstone with his supercharged TB.*

The greatest M.G. record-breaker

Once M.G. was making a healthy profit again, it was easier for Kimber to persuade Nuffield – Lord had left Morris Motors in 1936 after failing to agree on new terms – that record breaking and mud-plugging, as competition in the off-road trials was known, were commercially justifiable. He refused to let M.G. return to racing, but agreed to works support in other ventures provided it did not cost too much. So the Magic Magnette, EX135, was bought back from the Bellevue Garage team and fitted with a new streamlined body designed by Reid Railton, who was responsible for similar work on John Cobb's world land speed record-breaking car. The two Jacksons, and Enever, extracted even more power from its engine with the aid of a Zoller supercharger like the one used on the Magic Midget.

unit – with the VA gearbox's closer ratios. The new four-cylinder 1250 cc engine, code-named XPAG, was a much more modern design. It still had pushrods, but proved to be exceptionally well suited for tuning to give extra power. Because of its larger bore, the engine revved more easily and a lower rear axle ratio could be fitted, which together made the new TB much livelier than the TA. But unfortunately this attractive new model from M.G. was to be relatively short-lived, because war was already on the way.

Abingdon at war

The Abingdon workers were just as patriotic as everyone else in Britain: all they wanted to do was to join the military services or make fighting machines. But the slow-moving Nuffield Organization starved them of work and Kimber, with factory manager George 'Pop' Propert, obtained contracts independently from various government departments. They made all manner of things from frying pans to shell trays, and overhauled tanks and army trucks. But the Abingdon men were capable of far more, and they landed a contract to produce the main section of the Albemarle bomber. This large and intricate assembly had proved too formidable for three aircraft manufacturers – but Abingdon managed it, designing special tools and jigs besides taking on a large number of women workers to replace the men who had gone to war.

Activity of this nature was not really appreciated by the Nuffield Organization, which had always treated Abingdon as the Cinderella of its family of factories. Oliver Boden, who had taken over from Lord as managing director of Nuffield, died suddenly and was replaced by Miles Thomas. He was adamant that the group should be considered as one unit for producing armaments, with centralized control under one person: himself. So Thomas dismissed Kimber in November 1941 over the Albemarle issue.

Nevertheless, the aircraft contract proved to be a great success for M.G. and Abingdon went on to produce more bomber and tank equipment. Kimber, in the meantime, went to Charlesworth, the coachbuilders who had produced touring bodies for the SA. He spent 1942 reorganizing the factory for war work before moving on in 1943 to Specialloid Pistons in a similar capacity. In 1944, he was 56 years old and considering retirement when the war was over, or possibly even taking over as head of Triumph, to continue his policy of producing highly saleable sports cars from humble family saloon components. But, tragically, Kimber died in a London train crash in February 1945.

Sports cars again

One of the men who came back from the war was Lieutenant-Colonel John Thornley, who was service manager at Abingdon from 1934 to 1939 and had looked after the Cream Crackers and Musketeers. He got back his old job as service manager, with Propert continuing as general manager; but the old independence enjoyed under Kimber had been lost. Harold Ryder, who was rigidly opposed to all forms of motor sport, kept a firm control of Abingdon on behalf of Cowley.

However, Nuffield could not kill the spirit that flowed through Abingdon. Within weeks of the war ending this incredibly happy little factory was producing sports cars again. There was not time to design a new model and, in any case, the market was starved of new cars, because few manufacturers had survived in good enough fettle to meet the demand. Sports cars were even rarer, so the M.G. Midget sold extremely well. The first postwar machine, called the TC, was virtually the same as the TB, except that the rear suspension had been simplified and the width of the body increased to that of the Tickford coupé – which was discontinued – to give more elbow room inside.

Among the most affluent groups of people in Britain at that time were the American servicemen, paid at their home-country rates. With the

TC (1946)			
ENGINE		**CHASSIS**	
Type	M.G. in-line, water-cooled	Frame	Twin side members, cross members
No. of cylinders	4	Wheelbase mm	2388
Bore/stroke mm	66.5 x 90	Track – front mm	1143
Displacement cc	1250	Track – rear mm	1143
Valve operation	Overhead, pushrod	Suspension – front	Half-elliptic springs, beam axle
Sparkplugs per cyl.	1		
Compression ratio	7.5:1	Suspension – rear	Half-elliptic springs, live axle
Induction	Two SU carburettors		
BHP	54	Brakes	Drums all round
		Tyre size	19 x 4.50
DRIVE TRAIN		Wheels	Wire spoke
Clutch	Dry plate		
Transmission	Four-speed manual gearbox	**PERFORMANCE**	
		Maximum speed	126 km/h (78 mph)
		Acceleration	0-60 mph 22.7 sec.
		Fuel consumption	9.42 l/100 km (30 mpg)
		Number built	10.002

ABOVE *It mattered little that the M.G. TC was of distinctly prewar appearance when it went into production almost as soon as the war was over: it was a car that was available, rather than one that existed only in a manufacturer's brochure, as was the case with many of its potential rivals. This 1946 model, provided by Alastair Naylor, is owned by Derek Farley.*

LEFT *Abingdon was a hive of activity during the war, when large numbers of women workers were taken on to replace the men away fighting. Where once the almost frail-looking T series M.G.s had been produced, a variety of tanks appeared, including the Matildas pictured here in 1941. Another tank that could have borne the M.G. badge was the famous Crusader cruiser tank.*

thrills of war behind them, they turned to sports cars, and, in reality, there was only one new car available in any quantity: the M.G. TC. When their tours of duty were over, they took their new-found M.G.s home. Most Americans were astonished: they had never seen anything like it, a spindly little boneshaker that was seemingly indestructible and could run rings around their ponderous luxury liners. Why, it even made driving a pleasure rather than a chore!

The craze spread quickly, not only in America, but all over the world, so that when in 1947 Sir Stafford Cripps, President of the Board of Trade, cut steel supplies to any manufacturer who did not export enough, M.G. was in a good position. There was such a demand for the TC in America and the Commonwealth that Abingdon was able to get all the steel it needed. American dealers, in particular, were so anxious to buy M.G.s that the importers forced them to take two Volkswagens for every TC supplied. The importers made their profits on the Volkswagens, and the dealers sold the Volkswagens at a discount, making their money on the M.G.s! So, indirectly, Abingdon was responsible for helping to revive the German motor industry.

It was not practical to put the S, V and W ranges back into production in 1945. M.G. could sell as many TCs as it could make and Cripps was advocating a one-model policy for the austere postwar Britain. Another factor was that fuel was still severely rationed. Indeed for private motoring it disappeared altogether for eight months between 1947 and 1948. This made it even more pointless for M.G. to make a car that was

expensive to run, although it was worth producing an economic four-seater saloon and tourer.

Therefore, with an eye to the future, Abingdon resurrected a project that Enever had been working on with Cowley suspension designer Alec Issigonis in 1937. This was an M.G. version of the Morris Eight saloon, planned for introduction in 1941. The main advantage of its specification, apart from the fact that it had a single-carburettor version of the XPAG engine, was that it had an excellent new chassis with independent front suspension, a rarity at that time. Enever used Issigonis's wishbone and coil system, which was to become so popular in later years, rather than the torsion bars of the R-type. This new Y-type M.G., introduced in April 1947, was extraordinarily attractive and at first it sold well. Although Y-series production meant that Abingdon could turn out only 3500 TCs in 1949, the factory was happy because it meant that it was no longer dependent on one very aged model.

The Y-type, with its track of 1270 mm (4 ft 2 in) and substantial body, was rather heavy, but made up for this deficiency by having a very good ride, and by the ability of its engine to accept all the tuning gear that was being produced to make the TC go faster. An open touring version of the YA, as the new saloon was called, was designated the YT: it was introduced in October 1948, but looked bulky against the rakish TC and sold only in small numbers, mainly for export. Most of the production was for export, with Australia as the main market.

Meanwhile, the TCs went from strength to strength with all sorts of notable people being seen in them: the Duke of Edinburgh drove one before he married Princess Elizabeth, the future Queen, in 1947.

M.G. sales were going so well, at nearly 1700 in 1946, and rising fast to 5000 in 1949, that Ryder could see little reason for relaxing the ban on competition. However, Gardner's record-breaking car was privately owned and had survived the war, although its 1100 cc engine had not; there was little that Ryder could do to stop Gardner fitting it with a 750 cc engine – built at Abingdon before the war for an attack on Kohlrausch's record – and trying again.

The Jabbeke motorway between Ostend and Brussels proved ideal and Gardner smashed the record at 256.13 km/h (159.15 mph) in October 1946. In July the following year, with two of the six cylinders put out of action, he took the 500 cc record at 190 km/h (118.06 mph), also at Jabbeke. Help from Abingdon was very limited, however, with Jackson and Enever released only occasionally for competition work, so Gardner fitted a prototype 2-litre Jaguar engine to take the international class E record at 284.35 km/h (176.69 mph), again on the Belgian motorway, in September 1948. It is significant that William Lyons was willing to provide the power and collect the publicity, whereas Ryder was not. However, Gardner could not very well call his car a Jaguar, with its M.G. body and chassis, so he named it the Gardner Special.

Meanwhile, there had been a revolution at Cowley in 1947: Miles Thomas departed after a row with Lord Nuffield, and S.V. Smith took over from Ryder as the director in charge of Abingdon. Once more, with M.G. maintaining healthy profits, the ban on competition was relaxed a little.

Enever redesigned Gardner's M.G. Magnette-based record-breaking engine with a special crankshaft to run on three cylinders only in its 500 cc form; Gardner, his car once again called an M.G., recaptured the 500 cc record from the Italian Piero Taruffi with a 248.8 km/h (154.6 mph) run at Jabbeke in September 1949. Then its capacity was further reduced by cutting out yet another cylinder and Gardner took the 350 cc record with 194.87 km/h (121.09 mph) in Belgium in July 1950.

Riley moves in

The new Nuffield board had transferred production of one of M.G.'s erstwhile rivals, Riley, from Coventry to Abingdon in 1948 in the interests of rationalization. The little town in Berkshire (county changes have since placed it in Oxfordshire) was well on its way to having the world's biggest factory for the exclusive production of sporting cars. Two months after the arrival of the Rileys, Propert retired and was replaced by Riley general manager Jack Tatlow who, as luck would have it, got on extremely well with the Abingdon men.

The relatively cool reception for the YT, and the demands of the American dealers for something a little more sophisticated than the TC, convinced Tatlow and his new colleagues that another project should be designed. As ever, Abingdon was starved of investment – the available money all went into new head office models from Cowley – but it proved equal to the occasion. With Cecil Cousins and Syd Enever to the fore, the development men took out 127 mm (5 in) from the Y-type chassis centre section to give it a wheelbase of 2388 mm (7 ft 10 in) and fitted it with a hacked-about TC body. It was only then that the rough and ready prototype, duly approved by the Nuffield Organization, was sent to the drawing office at Cowley for plans to be prepared from which to produce it.

Cousins and company might have preferred to have produced something far more sophisticated, but the new car was just what was wanted: it had the potential for a soft, easy ride, and cost very little in

LEFT *The YT touring version of the M.G. TD is something of a rarity, with its body built more with comfort in mind than sporting appeal. It might have been overshadowed by the TD when it was new, but it has become something of a classic today as one of the last small family tourers. Provided by Ron Humphris.*

ABOVE RIGHT *The TD became the best-selling of the early M.G. Midgets. It consolidated the sales success pioneered by the TC because it was designed specifically for export markets. Its lines were acceptable when it was introduced in 1949, but they were already looking dated by the early 1950s as other manufacturers put completely new cars into production. Provided by Alastair Naylor, owned by Jack Tordoff.*

terms of time or money to develop. What is more, because it had the Y-type's advanced rack and pinion steering, it was easier to handle and, even more important for the Nuffield Organization and for Abingdon's fortunes, it could be readily converted to left-hand drive for export markets.

Although it had been decided that the new sports car's chassis would be basically the same as the Y-type saloon's, it had to be redesigned to a certain extent. The main problem was that there was not enough room at the back for adequate axle movement with the traditional underslung chassis members. Cowley got around this by sweeping up the side members over the rear axle so that the suspension could be made sufficiently supple to give an even ride with the shorter wheelbase and lighter two-seater body. The independent front suspension also made it necessary to fit new, smaller steel disc wheels in place of the delightful old wire ones used by the TC. Cowley really could not understand why people should be so in favour of the old-fashioned wire wheels, and, for once, they had the support of Thornley and Enever. Everyone admitted that wire wheels looked 'nostalgic' and racy, but they took a lot of work to keep clean and seldom looked good once they had left the showroom. But the real reason that wire wheels were not featured on the new model was that steel ones were cheaper to make and fitted in with the rest of the Nuffield range.

The new car's body was also widened by a further 102 mm (4 in) because of American demands, and looked considerably different once new wings had been designed to cover the wider track, new wheels and tyres. Bumpers (fenders) were also fitted at front and rear in deference to the American customers' wishes. The new model, designated the TD, was introduced in November 1949 and was to take Midget production to even greater heights. In 1950, Abingdon's total production exceeded 10,000 for the first time.

The relaxation of control at Abingdon had also enabled some

competition support to be given to private entrants using its products. Photographer George Phillips drove a modified TC with a low-drag body shaped rather like a cigar at Le Mans in 1949 and 1950, finishing runner-up in his class at the second attempt. In other events, a works team of three practically standard TDs was successful – it took the first three places in class and the team prize in the Tourist Trophy race in 1950.

The battle for a new car

It seemed incongruous that Phillips should race on with an outdated car, and therefore a new special was built for him, based on a tuned TD, for Le Mans in 1951. Apart from a higher-output engine, the main difference was that it was fitted with an open low-drag body to take advantage of the fast French circuit's long straight. The all-enveloping shape was similar to Gardner's car, and was so successful that the tuned TD showed itself to be capable of 190 km/h (120 mph) – nearly 80 km/h (50 mph) faster than the normal vehicle. The engine blew up in the race, but Enever, and Thornley, who had been appointed general manager in 1952 on Tatlow's retirement, were convinced that this should be the new M.G. to replace the TD.

Enever was not satisfied, however, because the driver and the passenger sat too high in the old-fashioned chassis, which had been intended for a narrow body with separate wings. His answer was to design a new chassis, with the side members spaced further apart so that the occupants could sit in between them, rather than on top of them. This was made possible by the use of a modern, all-enveloping body that cut down on the frontal area, which, in turn, reduced drag.

All looked well until the new car, called EX175, was presented for approval halfway through 1952, with a view to exhibiting it at the London Motor Show. Earlier that year, the Nuffield Organization had merged with Austin, Britain's other top motor manufacturer, to form

LEFT *A stunning overhead shot of one of the most famous M.G.s ever produced, the EX135 record-breaker, based on a 1934 K3 chassis, with its engine offset so that the driveline could run beside the driver rather than under him. The clear panels are used for display purposes only. Provided by BL Heritage Limited.*

ABOVE AND LEFT *The Y-type saloon was the first M.G. to go into production with independent front suspension – and was in great demand in immediate postwar years in a world starved of sporting cars. Its interior was also very comfortable. This 1953 YB model, provided by Jonathan Oglesby, is one of the last made.*

the British Motor Corporation. In theory, Lord Nuffield was in charge, but in effect the chief executive was his former right-hand man, Lord, who had joined Austin after leaving the Nuffield Organization. To Lord's credit, he was not prejudiced against M.G.s in particular; he just did not like sports cars. Nevertheless, he realized that BMC would have to produce them to make profits out of that sector of the market, but he did not see why there had to be more than one model. And only three days before he was shown EX175, Lord had been presented with a new model by Donald Healey. Healey, an independent manufacturer who had worked for Triumph before the war, had built a similar car to EX175, the Healey 100, using Austin components made redundant by the failure of Lord's Austin Atlantic sports coupé.

Lord had promptly concluded an agreement to produce Healey's car as the Austin-Healey 100 at Austin's works in Longbridge, Birmingham, on a royalty basis and so use up his embarrassing stockpile of Austin Atlantic engines and gearboxes. These plans were made public at the Motor Show in October 1952 and Lord told Thornley that he could shelve his car and carry on producing the TD.

Abingdon was dismayed. The TD, and the YB – a revised version of the Y-type saloon introduced late in 1951 with improved running gear – were selling well, but they were vulnerable because they were dated designs. The factory could see demand dropping off with the advent of the new Austin-Healey and the TR2, Triumph's similar new sports car. But Abingdon did what it could to keep M.G.'s reputation to the fore by

preparing a new supercharged TD-based engine for Gardner's record car. Enever raised its power output to an amazing 213 bhp that would have been enough to make the Gardner-M.G. capable of nearly 340 km/h (210 mph). But record attempts on the Bonneville Salt Flats in Utah in the United States during 1951 and 1952 ran into problems, so that the best achievement was several records broken and a single run at 325 km/h (202 mph). In the second session, Gardner spun, hitting his head on a marker post. He had to retire from competition after that, and it was the end of a glorious career for both man and car.

As a result of protests about changes in specification made to works racing TDs, a modified model had been offered from mid-1950. This was the Mark 2 fitted with a variety of works-approved tuning aids to make it go faster, although it was produced in only very small quantities. Thornley's worst fears were realized towards the end of 1952 when the demand for the TD started to fall away in America, its largest market. But still Lord would not lift his ban on EX175 because he was concerned that a modern M.G. would have taken sales away from the Austin-Healey 100.

Consequently Cousins and Enever went to work again to facelift the TD, doing it in an even simpler manner than they had achieved with the TC. No capital was available for development, or even the special tools needed for production, so they modified the TD's body to make it lower and sleeker along the lines of a new saloon (see next chapter) which was to be introduced at Abingdon to replace the antique YB. The more

TF1500 (1955)

ENGINE
Type	M.G. in-line, water-cooled
No. of cylinders	4
Bore/stroke mm	72 × 90
Displacement cc	1466
Valve operation	Overhead, pushrod
Sparkplugs per cyl.	1
Compression ratio	8.3:1
Induction	Two SU carburettors
BHP	63

DRIVE TRAIN
Clutch	Dry plate
Transmission	Four-speed manual

CHASSIS
Frame	Twin side members, cross members
Wheelbase mm	2388
Track – front mm	1203
Track – rear mm	1268
Suspension – front	Independent wishbone and coil
Suspension – rear	Half-elliptic springs, live axle
Brakes	Drums all round
Tyre size – front	5.50 × 15
Tyre size – rear	5.50 × 15
Wheels	Spoke or disc

PERFORMANCE
Maximum speed	142 km/h (88 mph)
Acceleration	0-60 mph 16 sec
Fuel consumption	12.28 litres/100 km (23 mpg)
Number built	3400

The M.G. TF was designed as a stopgap – but it turned out to be one of the prettiest cars Abingdon built and among the most desirable traditional sports cars. A 1955 1500 model provided by Alastair Naylor, owned by Vicki Fell.

LEFT *EX135 is shown at Bonneville in August 1951 on its last-but-one appearance after taking six international records, with its team behind it: from left to right, M.G. dealer and Gardner supporter Dick Benn, designer Syd Enever, driver and owner Goldie Gardner, tuning ace Reg Jackson, and electronics expert George Perry.*

BELOW LEFT *EX179, the car that took over from EX135, had a body of very similar shape that was to provide the basis for the new MGA. It also used a prototype MGA chassis, and a variety of MGA engines during its highly successful five-year career. Provided by BL Heritage Limited.*

RIGHT *Modern day record-breaker. Ron Gammons's ultra-lightweight (666 kg, 1467 lb) TF1500 competition model with 150 bhp was unbeaten in 2½ years of T-series racing – an extraordinarily long time bearing in mind the closeness of the competition. Provided by Brown and Gammons Ltd, owned by Ron Gammons.*

powerful TD Mark 2 engine was fitted and the new model called the TF (to avoid having people say 'Tee-Hee', which was likely if it had been called a TE). Wire wheels were also offered as an optional extra because the Austin-Healey 100 was equipped with them, and because enthusiasts never stopped clamouring for them. Just a few customers had managed to persuade the factory to fit wire wheels to the TD. Although it has since been accepted that the TF was one of the prettiest of the traditional 'square-rigged' M.G.s when it was launched in October 1953, it needed all the help it could get in competing against the more up-to-date Austin-Healey, Triumph and Volkswagen-based Porsches on the American market.

The second great M.G. record-breaker
It was at this time that the former driver of EX135, Captain George Eyston, managed to persuade BMC to build him another record car – and for old time's sake, and because Abingdon knew more about the business than anybody else, to make it a fully fledged M.G. Eyston's ideas also carried considerable weight with Lord because he was a director of the oil firm, Castrol, which would sponsor such a car. Eyston could not use the Gardner-M.G., even in revamped form, because it was the personal property of Gardner and, in any case, had been sponsored by a rival oil company, Duckham. At first, it was thought that Eyston could use EX175, duly modified with an undershield and tiny 'bubble' cockpit cover. But it proved unsuitable for use as a record car because its body was too closely related to a production vehicle and therefore produced too much drag. Fortunately, Enever had ordered a left-hand drive version of EX175's right-hand drive chassis at the time he was building the prototype, and this second frame was used for the new project, code-named EX179.

Gardner's M.G. had been fitted with highly supercharged versions of the XPAG engine, but for EX179 it was decided to go for a different set of records and take full advantage of the 1500 cc class limit by using a new enlarged engine, called the XPEG, without a supercharger. The 1466 cc capacity of this four-cylinder unit had been achieved by relocating the cylinders in joined or 'Siamese' (after the original Siamese twins) form so that the bores could be enlarged within the same overall external dimensions. Although this process has since become commonplace, it was considered quite revolutionary at the time. With the new engine installed in the spare chassis, and fitted with running gear and a body similar to the Gardner-M.G., EX179 took eight endurance records on the Utah salt flats in August 1954 at speeds of up to 247.34 km/h (153.69 mph).

It was essential to use the flats at that particular time because the salt was then in its best condition, but it also worked out very well for M.G. The venture by Eyston, with an American-based co-driver, Ken Miles, gained a lot of publicity for the new engine at a time when it was about to be installed in the TF. The 'record-breaking engine' was phased into the TF production lines towards the end of 1954 in an attempt to keep up sales while EX175 was at last developed for production.

The TF1500, as it was called, was a short-lived model. It stayed in production only until May 1955 before it was replaced by a new M.G., the MGA, but the TF1500 has since become the ultimate attraction for T-series enthusiasts as the fastest and most appealing of the line.

Meanwhile, EX179 was retained as the works record car, for Eyston, with Johnny Lockett, to achieve 16 international records up to 273.83 km/h (170.15 mph) at Utah in August 1956, when fitted with a prototype M.G. twin-cam engine. Nine more records up to 230.89 km/h (143.47 mph) were taken in August 1957, again at Utah, with another prototype M.G. engine, and – re-engined as an 'Austin-Healey' and called EX219 – a further 15 at Utah in September 1959! The drivers in 1957 were prewar ace Tommy Wisdom, David Ash and Phil Hill; in 1959, Wisdom, Ed Leavens and Gus Ehrmann. It mattered little who you put behind the wheel, or what you called it, EX179 was a real thoroughbred.

Boom-time at Abingdon

When the Nuffield Organization and the Austin Motor Company came together in 1952 to form the British Motor Corporation it was not so much a merger but rather, for practical purposes, a take-over by Austin. Lord Nuffield was 73 years old and, although he remained as president of BMC until his death in 1963, it was an honorary position. Leonard Lord, Austin's chairman and managing director, became the first to occupy this position at BMC, and he was in total charge. There is little doubt that he would have liked to have swept aside the Nuffield marques – Morris, Wolseley, Riley and M.G. – and produced only Austins in his new-found empire.

However, the Nuffield and Austin dealers had networks that often overlapped. If all BMC's products had carried the Austin label a large number of dealers would have lost their franchises, and there were so many of them that BMC could not have afforded the compensation. So Lord adopted an ingenious idea to get around the problem: 'badge engineering'. This meant that in future BMC would produce basic models which would be dressed up with different badges and trim as an Austin, Morris, or another relevant marque. Any small changes were welcome as long as they did not cost very much and helped to create the impression that the cars were indeed different. M.G.s did not fit in with this philosophy, and Lord was not keen on them as a result. But they were a necessary evil because of their magnificent sales record, so he decided that they could retain more of their individual identity, providing they were closely linked with at least one other car in the BMC range.

One of Lord's first moves in this programme of rationalization was to

PRECEDING PAGES *The first of the modern M.G. sports cars. The MGA brought wholesale changes to Abingdon and a vast expansion. This 1600 roadster, provided by Simon Robinson, is owned by Harold Corkhill.*

The new car, a four-seater with a wheelbase of 2591 mm (8 ft 6 in) and track of 1295 mm (4 ft 3 in), had independent front suspension and a live rear axle located by a torque arm. The torque arm was necessary because rubber bushes were used extensively in the suspension mountings to reduce noise, harshness and maintenance, which in turn made the little saloon altogether more civilized. As such, the car was an immediate success, particularly as the new engine made it much faster than the Wolseley, and such touches as an octagonal-like theme for the speedometer pleased people loyal to the marque. The new Magnette sold around 6000 a year, which was ten times as many as the YB saloon.

Its introduction was the start of a revolution at Abingdon, in which the little factory changed from being a works where cars were built from hundreds of small components to one where they were simply assembled, in much greater quantities, from a few large parts (such as the ready-trimmed bodyshells) which were made by outside suppliers.

The MGA prototypes

Once the new Magnette was well under way, Abingdon was given the go-ahead to produce EX175, the prototype for the new sports car to be known as the MGA. This went against the grain with Lord because he had given virtually all design authority to Austin's office at Longbridge, but there was sound commercial sense in letting M.G. produce its own car now that the Midget was on the way out. The new M.G. would use the Austin B-series running gear and needed only a body and chassis that were already developed and could be produced within BMC or by its established suppliers; and the American sports car market had

ABOVE *The car that started it all: George Phillips's Le Mans special with the EX135-inspired bodywork that was to form the basis for the MGA.*

axe Nuffield's engines. The Morris Minor's unit was replaced by an A-series engine from the Austin A30 and, in 1954, the Morris Oxford received an enlarged, 1489 cc version of the Austin A40's B-series four-cylinder engine. Later, the big cars – the Austin Westminster and the Morris Isis – were powered by the same 2.6-litre six-cylinder Austin C-series engine.

The new Magnette

At the same time, Lord started standardizing the bodyshells. The Wolseley 4/44, which had been launched in 1952 with the XPAG 1250 cc engine, was modified to take the B-series unit and M.G. grille and badges. For this new Z-series M.G. introduced in October 1953, M.G. resurrected the name Magnette, which had not been used since 1936. Despite its close relationship to the 4/44 – Wolseley models had for so long formed the basis of M.G.s – it was completely unlike any previous M.G. It was a pleasing Italian-styled saloon of unitary construction – i.e. it had no separate chassis, the bodyshell providing mountings for the engine, gearbox and suspension. This form of construction was rapidly becoming popular in the early 1950s as a far lighter and, when mass-produced, cheaper way of making cars. One of the advantages of the system was that the passengers were able to sit lower – thus improving handling and reducing drag – because they did not have chassis rails under them; just a flat floorpan on which the bodyshell was based.

50

expanded so much that there was room for a 1.5-litre Austin-Healey, and Jaguar's 3.4-litre XK. BMC had also been persuaded to set up a competitions department following the success (and sales) enjoyed by Jaguar as a result of racing, and by Triumph in rallying. Abingdon was the obvious place to establish the department, because Lord had plans to turn the works into his sports car centre – and, in any case, it was where all the enthusiasm, skill and specialized knowledge were located. Donald Healey's company at Warwick was closer to Longbridge, but it had never been on a par with Abingdon.

With this welcome change of attitude at BMC in 1955, Thornley very shrewdly planned to announce the new sports car, the MGA, at the beginning of June and then run three of them at Le Mans a few days later. Unfortunately the body tooling took longer than expected and the Le Mans entries were taken up by three prototypes bearing the designation EX182. These cars were almost exactly the same as the actual MGA, with the chassis used in Eyston's 240 km/h (150 mph) record car the year before, and a body based on the 1951 Le Mans car, which could trace its ancestry to the Gardner-M.G. The engine and running gear, which were basically similar to those used in the Magnette, had already been developed in saloon car racing.

RIGHT *The name Magnette was carried on to M.G.'s first car of unitary construction, the ZA saloon. This 1956 model is an interim version using the later ZB mechanical components. Provided by Warren Marsh.*

MGA 1600 (1959)	
ENGINE	
Type	M.G. in-line, water-cooled
No. of cylinders	4
Bore/stroke mm	75.4 x 88.9
Displacement cc	1588
Valve operation	Overhead, pushrod
Sparkplugs per cyl.	1
Compression ratio	8.3:1
Induction	Two SU carburettors
BHP	79.5
DRIVE TRAIN	
Clutch	Dry plate
Transmission	Four-speed manual
CHASSIS	
Frame	Twin side members, cross members
Wheelbase mm	2388
Track – front mm	1203
Track – rear mm	1230
Suspension – front	Independent wishbone and coil
Suspension – rear	Half-elliptic springs, live axle
Brakes	Discs front, drums rear
Tyre size – front	5.60 x 15
Tyre size – rear	5.60 x 15
Wheels	Wire spoke or steel disc
PERFORMANCE	
Maximum speed	166 km/h (103 mph)
Acceleration	0-60 mph 13.3 sec.
Fuel consumption	10.1 litres/100 km (28 mpg)
Number built	31,501

ABOVE *The early MGA had a clean shape with no door handles, a throwback to the days when sports cars rarely had hoods fitted. In bad weather you opened the door on this 1600 roadster through a flap in the sidescreen. Provided by Simon Robinson; owner H. Corkhill.*

ABOVE *Line-up for Le Mans in 1955 – from the left, the prototype MGAs of Lockett and Miles (number 41), Jacobs and Flynn (number 42), Lund and Waeffler (number 64).*

The three new M.G.s were running well in the 1955 Le Mans until everything was overshadowed by motor racing's worst accident in which 82 people were killed as a Mercedes-Benz collided with an Austin-Healey and flew into the crowd. In the confusion following the crash M.G. stalwart Dick Jacobs also crashed and nearly lost his life. But the remaining two M.G.s ran better than expected to finish 12th and 17th in the hands of Ken Miles and Johnny Lockett, and Ted Lund and Hans Waeffler.

The prototypes had been built with a view to running soon after in the Alpine Rally, but this event was one of the many cancelled in 1955 in the aftermath of Le Mans. Nevertheless, it was planned to enter the EX182 cars in the Tourist Trophy at Dundrod in September to coincide with the MGA's new launch date. Because the new car would then be a reality, two of the EX182 cars were fitted with twin-cam development

engines and the third, the Le Mans spare, retained the original pushrod unit. In this way, Abingdon felt that it could demonstrate that not only did it have a fast new car, but even greater performance could be achieved with the more powerful twin-cam engines.

One of the new twin-cam conversions on the B-series unit had been developed by Austin and the other by the Morris engine works, but when both gave trouble in practice it was decided to go ahead with only the Austin. A spare pushrod engine replaced the Morris unit. The car that retained its twin-cam engine, driven by Lockett and Ron Flockhart, was also fitted with experimental disc brakes and low-drag bodywork. It proved to be practically as fast as the class-winning Porsche before retiring with head gasket trouble. One of the pushrod cars also failed to finish because of a split fuel tank, but the other, driven by Jack Fairman and Peter Wilson, survived to finish 20th, a lap ahead of the Triumph

TR2s. This race, too, was marred by tragedy as three drivers died in horrifying accidents.

The death toll was giving motor racing a bad name in Europe and BMC decided to concentrate on rallying, in which its near-standard cars would have a better chance of success in any case, and to develop the Morris version of the twin-cam engine as it was more closely related to the B-series unit.

The MGA in production and in competition

It was in this stern atmosphere that the MGA was launched as an open tourer, with spartan equipment, a very low price and a top speed of nearly 160 km/h (100 mph). The body was made entirely from steel in the interests of mass production, rather than aluminium like the prototypes. Wire wheels were also offered as an option to the cheaper steel disc wheels, M.G. having learned its lesson in that area. The MGA, with its superbly safe handling, high top speed and good fuel consumption of around 9.4 litres/100 km (30 mpg), was an immediate sales success, the vast majority of cars going to America, as before. The tragedies of Le Mans and the TT had not had such an impact across the Atlantic, so BMC allowed its North American subsidiary to enter three MGAs in the Sebring 12-hour race. They won the team prize and helped start a tradition: BMC sent works teams of sports cars to the event for more than 10 years.

Team cars also raced in the Mille Miglia in 1956 – Abingdon assured BMC that it was more of a rally than a road race! – and in the Alpine

BELOW *Ted Lund campaigned a Twin Cam MGA with works support at Le Mans in 1959, 1960 and 1961. Following a crash in 1959, it was fitted with special streamlined hardtop bodywork, and finished 12th in 1960. Engine trouble eliminated it in 1961. Provided by R.D. McElroy.*

Rally. The works MGAs ran with hard tops in the Alpine event, not only because they made the cars less tiring to drive, but also because, after Le Mans, the French government had barred sports cars from road rallies. This resulted in thinly disguised sports cars running as GT machines with hard tops in place!

Meanwhile, Abingdon was developing a fixed-head coupé version of the MGA along the lines of Jaguar's popular XK fixed-head. This poor man's Jaguar, with a more luxurious interior than previous M.G.s, glass side windows and a slightly higher top speed because of its superior aerodynamics, was introduced at the London Motor Show in October 1956. At the same time, the Magnette, which had progressed to a ZB with a higher-output engine when the original MGA was launched, appeared in its final form, as the Varitone with a two-tone colour scheme and a larger, more modern rear window.

Works MGAs and Magnettes enjoyed a great deal of success in rallying, particularly when driven by Nancy Mitchell, who used them to win the European ladies' championship in 1956 and 1957.

Transition and expansion

The mid-1950s were a time of great expansion for Abingdon as MGA production rose to 20,000 a year and the more traditional RM Rileys were phased out to be replaced by badge-engineered versions built at Cowley. The Rileys' place at Abingdon was taken by M.G.'s rival, the Austin-Healey, manufacture of which moved there in late 1956, to make this the world's most productive factory devoted entirely to sports cars.

Thornley summed up these years of transition as the most dramatic for Abingdon:

'Up to 1952, Abingdon produced 250 vehicles a week all-out. By 1956, it was producing 1300 from very much the same floor space.'

When we were producing 250 T types a week, I suppose we possibly employed 550 to 600 people all-up, of which, perhaps, 200 were the irreducible minimum of admin. That meant that you had around 400 work people and foremen. By the time we were building 1300 vehicles a week, we had 1300 employees and made some play of "one vehicle per person per week: match that anybody else if you can". But, of course, we bought the vehicles in such enormous chunks that it wasn't very highly labour intensive.

'On the design side, we did everything first and presented it as a *fait accompli*. Why I didn't get kicked all the way from here to Birmingham and back, I cannot imagine, but I did this constantly. There were major confrontations as a result, but no recriminations for having done so. By the time it was done they were always very delighted.

LEFT AND BELOW *Enever's last great record-breaker, EX181, was of very advanced design for 1957. It featured a mid-mounted engine in a spaceframe with a de Dion rear axle that owed a great deal to an abortive attempt at building a world-beating sports racing car. Its aircraft-style teardrop shape was more efficient than the earlier cars. EX181 is shown at Bonneville with Phil Hill, and with its cockpit canopy removed. Provided by BL Heritage Limited.*

'The major confrontations were concerned with threats to close the plant and shift production elsewhere. I fought a number of battles on those lines.

'On record breaking, we took it to the point where it would have been foolish to cancel and step back, and I then went forward and said I wanted £5000 to go to Utah and that sort of thing. We did a lot of skating on thin ice one way or another. What an exciting life it was!'

Meanwhile, EX179 had been used as part of the development programme for the twin-cam engine during its record run in August 1956 before a new record car, EX181, was built to take the engine in 1957. Nevertheless, EX179 was retained to help develop the A-series engine for a new small Austin-Healey sports car, the Sprite. EX181 was a tiny teardrop-shaped car based on a tubular frame designed by Enever. M.G. realized that this lighter and more rigid type of chassis would be needed if it was to keep in the forefront of sports car racing. In the event it was too expensive to make, but EX181 proved ideal for developing the new twin-cam engine, which was intended to give the MGA a good performance in production car racing. With Stirling Moss at the wheel, and a supercharged version of the twin-cam installed, EX181 broke five international records, achieving 395.32 km/h (245.64 mph) at Utah during the 1957 session with EX179.

MGA Twin Cam (1960)

ENGINE		CHASSIS	
Type	M.G. in-line four-cylinder	**Frame**	Twin side members, cross members
No. of cylinders	4	**Wheelbase mm**	2388
Bore/stroke mm	75 × 89	**Track – front mm**	1203
Displacement cc	1588	**Track – rear mm**	1230
Valve operation	Overhead, chain-driven twin camshafts	**Suspension – front**	Independent wishbone and coil
Sparkplugs per cyl.	1	**Suspension – rear**	Half elliptic springs, live axle
Compression ratio	9.9:1 or 8.3:1	**Brakes**	Discs all round
Induction	Two SU carburettors	**Tyre size – front**	5.90 × 15
BHP	108	**Tyre size – rear**	5.90 × 15
		Wheels	Steel disc centre-lock
DRIVE TRAIN		**PERFORMANCE**	
Clutch	Dry plate	**Maximum speed**	182 km/h (113 mph)
Transmission	Four-speed manual. Optional four-speed manual with close-ratio gears	**Acceleration**	0-60 mph 9.9 sec
		Fuel consumption	14.12 litres/100 km (20 mpg)
		Number built	2111

The Twin Cam MGA and the 1600 Mark II

This notable success gave Abingdon the boost it needed to introduce the twin-cam engine in a new MGA, alongside the existing models in July 1958. The Twin Cam cars, as they were called, available with open or closed bodywork, were also fitted with Dunlop disc brakes all round to cope with the extra performance of the engine, which had been bored out to 1588 cc to take full advantage of the 1600 cc international competition classes. The power output of 108 bhp, against the normal engine's 72, gave the new car far better acceleration and a high top speed of 182 km/h (113 mph), although fuel consumption increased to 14.12 litres/100 km (20 mpg).

The Twin Cam was not a great success, however, either in competition or in production. On the track, it was usually outclassed by far more specialized and expensive machinery, although works cars did well in national GT events; in rallying, BMC concentrated on the Austin-Healey because, with its engine enlarged to 3 litres, it stood a better chance of overall victory. In everyday use, the Twin Cam engine suffered from oil consumption problems – which were eventually cured – and the need for a higher standard of service than was readily available, particularly in the United States where such power units in low-priced cars were rare.

As a result, only just over 2000 Twin Cams were made before the model was discontinued in 1960; redundant chassis were used to produce a rare hybrid known as the De Luxe, in effect a Twin Cam with a pushrod engine of which only limited quantities were made.

Meanwhile, as Abingdon production soared to more than 40,000 cars a year with the introduction of the new small Austin-Healey, the Sprite, the Magnette Varitone – selling better than ever – was replaced in 1959 by a badge-engineered version of Austin's wallowing Cambridge 1½-litre saloon: the Magnette Mark III. This family four-seater M.G., with a massive body designed by the Italian firm of Farina, was not even built at Abingdon. It was entirely the brainchild of Longbridge.

Abingdon's disappointment at losing the Varitone was mollified by an improvement in the MGA's specification. The capacity of the engine was increased in July 1959 to that of the Twin Cam and disc brakes were fitted at the front. This was the MGA 1600, which was to be relatively short-lived. The engine's capacity was increased again in April 1961 to 1622 cc by means of a longer stroke. This was logical because it made it the same as the Farina-bodied BMC saloons, including the Magnette. The new MGA was designated the 1600 Mark II, and the older 1600 subsequently became known as the Mark I.

It was during this run that MGA production passed 100,000, a historic achievement for such a small factory. Meanwhile, EX181 was still active – Phil Hill used it to take six more international records at Utah with 408.77 km/h (254.91 mph) in September 1959 – alongside the revamped EX179, now designated EX219. Although factory involvement with the MGA in competition from 1957 was minimal, Abingdon supported a special version driven by Lund in the 1959 Le Mans race but he was eliminated by gearbox trouble. However, Lund and Colin Escott had better luck in 1960, when the car was fitted with a special hard top to complement new windscreen regulations, and took 12th place. Sebring continued to be a happy hunting ground for Abingdon: in 1960 Austin-Healeys and MGAs did well, and a De Luxe coupé won its class. In fact, it performed so successfully that the BMC works team prepared one for rallying in 1961, and with it the Morley brothers, Don and Erle, won their class in the Monte Carlo Rally, before the Finn Rauno Aaltonen and the Swede Gunnar Palm repeated the trick in the Tulip Rally. It was a glorious swansong for a car that was to be replaced late in 1962 by the far more modern MGB, which was to become the best-selling M.G. of all.

LEFT *Mike Ellman-Brown collected the last MGA Twin Cam to be made from the factory in June 1960 and still owns the car today. It was specially finished for him in 'woodland green', showing that Abingdon never lost its human touch despite the massive expansion of those days.*

ABOVE *The fixed-head coupé bodywork on the MGA chassis represented John Thornley and Syd Enever's tilt at the sophisticated GT market formerly dominated by far more expensive cars such as Aston Martin, Jaguar, Alfa Romeo and Porsche. The M.G.'s lines were pleasing and the car sold well. A 1960 Mark II MGA fixed-head coupé provided by Mrs Jill Halfpenny.*

RIGHT *Following the demise of the Twin Cam, surplus chassis were used up to make a rare and unpublicized model, the Mark II De Luxe, one of which – with a highly tuned pushrod engine – proved very successful in international rallying. The 1961 MGA 1600 De Luxe Mark II rally car was provided by Mike Harrison.*

Cars
by the million

The credit for M.G.'s greatest landmark, the day on which production passed a million, must fall to John Thornley, who re-established a design office at Abingdon in 1954 with Syd Enever in charge. As we know, one of Enever's first jobs was to put EX175 into production as the MGA. Various other projects followed, including the EX181 record-breaking car, which was to inspire the MGA's successor, and work on improving the Austin-Healey Sprite, which went into production at Abingdon in May 1958. The tiny Austin-Healey, with its running gear made from a combination of BMC A-series, Morris Minor and M.G. parts, was a spiritual successor to the M.G. Midget even if it did bear a rival marque's name. BMC managing director George Harriman, who had succeeded Lord on his retirement in 1956, saw no reason why the Sprite should not be badge-engineered as an M.G. Midget, so that it could be sold through the old Nuffield chain of dealers as well as the existing Austin outlets.

However, first the car needed a certain amount of development: it had a curious bonnet with high-mounted headlights resembling frog's eyes, no exterior bootlid, and quarter-elliptic rear springs that led to some instability. BMC's solution was to give the job of redesigning the front to Healey and the back to Enever! The exact reasons for this extraordinary decision have been lost in the mists of time, but in the event Enever and Healey's designers got together to produce the Austin-Healey Sprite Mark II in July 1961 with an M.G. Midget – known as the Mark I – version at a slightly higher price, but including a different grille and more chromium plating. It was decided that the boost to marketing offered by the new bodywork was more important than the rear suspension, so Enever's solution of half-elliptic springs was shelved.

The Sprite, with its economical 948 cc four-cylinder engine, top speed of 137 km/h (85 mph), short wheelbase of 2032 mm (6 ft 8 in), and very low price, had been selling at around 17,000 a year. With the introduction of the M.G. Midget version of the car, sales climbed to a total of 18,000 a year, with slightly more M.G.s sold than Austin-Healeys: enough to justify the badge engineering for BMC.

Happily, the appearance of the new M.G. Midget fitted in well with the shape of the MGA's replacement, the MGB, which Enever had been working on for more than four years. Although EX181 was mid-engined, he used the car's body as the inspiration for the new MGB. The tubular frame used in EX181 had to be abandoned on the grounds of cost, and therefore a way had to be found to make the car more rigid. This was necessary so that it could use a modern soft suspension system to give it a better ride without a deterioration in handling. Only in this way could the MGA be improved upon without drastic changes in the established mechanical components. BMC had other running gear on the drawing board, but it seemed unlikely that it would be much better than the old B-series parts.

Enever had little choice but to pursue the same line of approach to unitary construction as was taken on the Sprite. At first he tried to devise an independent rear suspension system, but it could not be made cheaply enough, so he tried coil springs and radius arms. The same fate befell that system, and he had to settle for half-elliptic leaf springs as intended for the Sprite and Midget. The rest of the MGB's monocoque was similar in principle to the new Midget in that it was based on a floorpan with substantial box section sills, but it was considerably stronger. Wonders had been achieved by paring down the wheelbase from 2388 mm (7 ft 10 in) to 2311 mm (7 ft 7 in), because the EX181-styled body was too bulbous in prototypes built around the MGA's frame. This marginal alteration in size – which was achieved without reducing the room available for the occupants – also helped to save weight. And because of the way in which it was done, it left plenty of room in the engine compartment for alternative power units should they become available.

PRECEDING PAGES *The MGB stayed in production far longer than expected and, because of its inherent good design, sold in vast numbers all over the world. This is one of the last roadsters to be built, in 1980. Provided by Performance Cars Ltd.*

RIGHT *Although based on an earlier Austin-Healey, the modern M.G. Midget was a worthy successor to the more traditional cars, as it was made from well-proven components to provide safe and economical motoring for those not attracted by family saloons. Production went on for an almost unprecedented length of time, and huge sales resulted. A 1963 Mark I provided by J.A. Tassell.*

Midget (1963)	
ENGINE	
Type	M.G. in-line, water-cooled
No. of cylinders	4
Bore/stroke mm	65 × 84
Displacement cc	1098
Valve operation	Overhead, pushrod
Sparkplugs per cyl.	1
Compression ratio	8.9:1
Induction	Two SU carburettors
BHP	56
DRIVE TRAIN	
Clutch	Dry plate
Transmission	Four-speed manual
CHASSIS	
Frame	Unitary
Wheelbase mm	2030
Track – front mm	1160
Track – rear mm	1140
Suspension – front	Independent wishbone and coil
Suspension – rear	Quarter-elliptic springs, live axle
Brakes	Discs front, drums rear
Tyre size – front	5.20 × 13
Tyre size – rear	5.20 × 13
Wheels	Wire spoke or steel disc
PERFORMANCE	
Maximum speed	142 km/h (88 mph)
Acceleration	0-60 mph 18 sec
Fuel consumption	8.07 litres/100 km (35 mpg)
Number built	9601

MGB (1967)	
ENGINE	
Type	M.G. in-line, water-cooled
No. of cylinders	4
Bore/stroke mm	80 × 89
Displacement cc	1798
Valve operation	Overhead, pushrod
Sparkplugs per cyl.	1
Compression ratio	8.8:1
Induction	Two SU carburettors
BHP	95
DRIVE TRAIN	
Clutch	Dry plate
Transmission	Four-speed manual, gearbox or manual and overdrive
CHASSIS	
Frame	Unitary
Wheelbase mm	2311
Track – front mm	1245
Track – rear mm	1250
Suspension – front	Independent wishbone and coil
Suspension – rear	Half-elliptic springs, live axle
Brakes	Discs front, drums rear
Tyre size – front	5.60 × 14
Tyre size – rear	5.60 × 14
Wheels	Wire spoke or steel disc
PERFORMANCE	
Maximum speed	171 km/h (106 mph)
Acceleration	0-60 mph 12.5 sec
Fuel consumption	10.46 litres/100 km (27 mpg)
Number built	137,733

ABOVE AND RIGHT *The Mark I
MGB was a sturdy, straight-
forward sports car with features
that will fascinate enthusiasts
in the future. In the early 1960s
slatted radiator grilles were common,
as were beautifully engineered
toggle switches and pillars for
adjusting mirror height. A 1967
roadster provided by E.F. Williams.*

Despite their ingenuity, the M.G. designers ran into what was to be a common problem with unitary construction. To make the new bodyshell sufficiently rigid, they had to use so much steel that it was heavier than the old body and chassis units combined. The final development in paring down the weight without sacrificing rigidity or strength would have cost a great deal of time and money, and Abingdon just could not afford it. As it was, Thornley had to 'adjust' the price of the new bodyshell by getting the Pressed Steel Company – which was to make it – to agree to a lower price for the very expensive initial tooling, with a higher figure for each complete bodyshell as compensation. Ironically, when for a variety of reasons MGB production went on for far longer than expected – more than 500,000 were made – Pressed Steel gained enormously from this arrangement. With hindsight, BMC would have been better to have given unqualified backing to brilliant managers such as Thornley, who had no option but to go for unitary construction in view of the overall savings in money, and the technical improvement.

Because the MGB was turning out to be heavier than the MGA, it was decided to uprate the engine so that the performance did not suffer. This was achieved by increasing the capacity to 1798 cc with an enlarged bore and the 'Siamezing' techniques established on the XPEG in 1954. The new M.G. roadster even had locks on the doors and bootlid, plus proper door handles, items the MGA had lacked! Thornley said later:

'I remember a time when Syd and I sat down for an hour-and-a-quarter with a 21p door lock in one hand and a 19p one in the other, wondering which one we could afford. Over the years we had processions of people saying: "Why don't you do this or that – it will cost only a few pence". By the time you have added up all those pennies you've put £20 on the price of the car, and – with purchase tax – you are halfway to the same price as your nearest rival.'

Sales bonanza

However, Enever and Thornley had done their arithmetic so well that the MGB was introduced in September 1962, in roadster form only, at a cheaper price than any rival, despite having comparable fittings such as wind-up windows in place of floppy sidescreens, and the locks and door handles. Sports cars were getting altogether more civilized and, with the MGB to the fore, sales went up and up, especially in America where the customers appreciated a little extra refinement.

The MGB was only part of BMC's success in the early 1960s. The revolutionary front-wheel drive Mini, introduced in 1959, had dominated the small car market and for some time an M.G. version had been planned. However, the specialist racing car manufacturer, John Cooper, was on the crest of a wave, having won the constructors' world championship twice, and he sold his own version of the Mini, the Mini-Cooper, to BMC. When it was produced in both Austin and Morris forms to cash in on the Cooper name, it put paid to any ideas about a badge-engineered, higher-performance, M.G. Mini. Abingdon also spent a lot of time developing two-seater sports versions of the Mini before the designs were rejected. This was because many people, including the Mini's designer, Alec Issigonis, did not think that front-wheel-drive was suitable for sports cars and pointed out that a two-seat configuration did not make efficent use of the cabin space available in a Mini.

However, BMC wanted a small saloon to market as an M.G. alongside the Magnette, which had progressed to a Mark IV with a variety of subtle changes in September 1961. The need was especially

standard but were better streamlined and weighed less, were prepared at Abingdon for Dick Jacobs to enter in the popular British GT championship. These cars had racing A-series engines of various capacities from 948 cc to 1293 cc (depending on what was allowed by individual regulations) and won their class in numerous events, plus the 1963 *Autosport* championship when driven by Andrew Hedges and Alan Foster. They were also first and second in their class in the 1964 Nürburgring 1000-kilometre race – but most of the Spridget racing effort was undertaken by the Donald Healey Motor Company, which had been involved at an earlier point with the Mark I Sprite.

Nevertheless, BMC was anxious to promote the M.G. version of the Spridget, particularly in America, and provided a Midget for Peter Riley and Mike Hughes to win their class in the 1962 Sebring 12-hour race. They even badge-engineered one of the successful Sebring Sprite special coupés as an M.G. for Graham Hill in the 1963 event, but unfortunately the car had to retire with final drive problems. BMC would have liked to have done the same thing with the M.G. 1100, but – although a Jacobs-entered example won its class in the 1962 Brands Hatch six-hour saloon car race, and the odd 1100 appeared in rallies – the model was simply not competitive alongside the smaller, lighter, and highly manoeuvrable Mini-Cooper with its stiffer suspension.

The MGB might have been overweight for international competition, but it had the advantage of years of development on the B-series mechanical components. In 1963, three works MGBs were raced with moderate success in the long-distance events in which reliability was of paramount importance, and in the *Autosport* championship. Alan

LEFT *Badge engineering was at its extreme when the BMC Farina-styled saloons were introduced. A 1966 M.G. Magnette Mark IV provided by the Pre-War M.G. Parts Centre.*

BELOW LEFT *The M.G. 1100 was a similar badge-engineering exercise using a basic BMC saloon to make an M.G. Provided by Joyce Mitchell.*

RIGHT *The works ran near-standard MGBs at Le Mans until increasing specialization rendered them ineligible. Apart from tuning, the main alteration was the new nose. Hutcheson and Hopkirk are shown finishing 12th in 1963.*

evident in America, where M.G.s had acquired a great reputation, so BMC produced a badge-engineered sporting version of its Austin/Morris 1100 – the next step up from a Mini, and one step below the rather over-bodied Farina 1489 cc saloons such as Magnette. The 1100 was an outstanding success from its introduction in September 1962, rapidly becoming Britain's top-selling car, with the M.G. versions initially at the top of the range. The basic 1100 offered more comfortable accommodation for four people than the Mini, with advanced Hydrolastic fluid suspension and a similar performance because it had a larger, 1098 cc, A-series engine. The M.G. 1100 had a twin carburettor version of the engine, giving it a top speed of 142 km/h (88 mph), and was available mainly in two-door form as befitted its sporting image.

This new A-series engine with its larger bore and stroke was also fitted to the Midget and Sprite, with disc brakes at the front to cope with the extra performance. The Mark I and Mark II designations were retained for the Midget and Sprite respectively, although many enthusiasts ignored all distinctions and called the cars Spridgets.

Although the BMC competitions department, and the Cooper Car Company, concentrated principally on the Mini-Cooper, which stood a good chance of overall victory in international rallies and thrilled the crowds with tyre-smoking attacks on corners in circuit racing, the new range of M.G.s was given the opportunity to prove itself in competition. Two special Midgets, with aluminium fastback bodies that looked fairly

Hutcheson was second in his class in the *Autosport* series behind Dickie Stoop's far more expensive Porsche Carrera, and, despite spending 85 minutes digging the car out of the sand at the end of the Mulsanne Straight, again finished second in class to a prototype Porsche 718/8 Spyder at Le Mans. This MGB was slightly modified from normal competition specification as it was fitted with a low-drag nose, taking it nearer to the shape of EX181. This nose was removed three months later for the Tour de France, a fast road race-cum-rally, in which Hedges and John Sprinzel held down fourth place before crashing. Private entrants Patrick Vanson and Roger Derolland made amends by taking a brand-new MGB, fitted with various options and tuning equipment that anyone could buy, to seventh place overall.

The tough, practical and, most important, cheap Midgets and MGBs became extremely popular for private entrants in all forms of motoring sport: Ronnie Bucknum enjoyed years of success whith his Hollywood Sports Cars MGB in Sports Car Club of America events, and Bill Nicholson started a career in a 1963 car that was still continuing nearly 20 years later!

It was also during 1963 that an overdrive was offered as an option on the road-going MGB. This immediately became popular as it allowed far more relaxed high-speed cruising with greater economy, although it was withheld from the American market for a while because it was thought that the MGB in this form might further demolish the dwindling sales of the Austin-Healey 3000. Despite the low-key works

involvement with the MGB, the Morley brothers, who had startled so many people with their performance in the MGA De Luxe in 1961, again won the GT category in an MGB in the 1964 Monte Carlo Rally. However, most of the publicity was scooped by Hutcheson's 1963 Le Mans partner, Paddy Hopkirk, who won the event outright in a Mini-Cooper S. With Hedges, Hopkirk was back behind the wheel of a long-nose MGB at Le Mans in 1964, where it finished sixth in class behind no fewer than five Porsche 904s. However, the new Porsches looked far more like racing cars than sports cars, so the MGB gained valuable publicity, particularly as it reached 224 km/h (139 mph) along the Mulsanne Straight and averaged 160.77 km/h (99.9 mph) overall. As Thornley was to point out, 99.9 mph was even better in terms of publicity than 100 mph! In addition, the MGB won the *Motor* trophy for the highest-placed British car, with 19th overall.

The new Spridgets

Despite the Spridget's competition record, which was excellent compared with that of its rivals, particularly in the same low price bracket, these cars were looking decidedly dated by 1964. They still had sidescreens and their ride was far too bumpy because of the limited

axle travel allowed by the quarter-elliptic rear suspension. So they were revised as the Mark II Midget and the Mark III Sprite in March 1964 with new wind-up windows and Enever's half-elliptic rear suspension, which not only gave them a softer ride but made them feel more stable. The engine's output was also increased from 55 to 59 bhp, which produced a top speed of 153 km/h (95 mph), with improved acceleration.

Soon after, in September 1964, the MGB was given a more up-to-date B-series engine with five main bearings rather than three, but there were no significant changes to the best-selling range until October 1965. This was the date when the famous fixed-head MGB GT was introduced.

Thornley was very keen on the GT – which, with its hatchback rear door, he likened to an Aston Martin DB Mark III – because he felt that it would increase the MGB's sales potential dramatically. But he did not get all his own way, because he would have preferred to have had the job done properly with a large amount of weight removed from the bottom structure to compensate for the extra weight of the steel roof. The stressed top would have made up for the loss of rigidity from lightening the bottom. However, BMC, still involved in a cut-throat

Clubman such as Barry Sidery-Smith continue to race MGBs in a form little altered from the early 1960s. The only noticeable difference on his 1966 car is in the use of modern slick tyres and a later spoiler.

price war with Triumph and with numerous other models to revise, opted for the cheapest alternative in terms of development costs, fitting an Austin A40-style angular top to the rounded roadster's bottom.

It is to Enever's eternal credit that he managed to blend the contrasting styles together so well, although he had no opportunity to lighten the shell overall. Considering that it was developed with such economy, the GT was an extremely compact and efficient design. Its roof was slightly higher than the detachable hard top which had been introduced for the roadster in 1963, and the windows were larger. There was a good-sized platform for luggage behind two tiny rear seats that were just big enough for children of up to about 8 years old. In this way the range of potential customers for the MGB was increased considerably.

The works continued to race MGBs in the lighter roadster form, with the detachable hard top in place to qualify the cars as GTs! They continued to perform well in events such as the Sebring 12 hours, but they struggled to qualify at Le Mans in 1964, which showed how their overall weight kept down their top speed. However, the MGB's great reliability stood it in good stead for Britain's longest postwar race, the Brands Hatch 1000-mile in 1965. The privately entered works car of

John Rhodes and Warwick Banks was slower than many of the other contestants, such as a 4.2-litre Jaguar E type, but it used fewer tyres on the tight Kentish circuit and won by seven laps, with three other MGBs in the first 12 places. At Le Mans in 1965, Hopkirk and Hedges managed to qualify a new works car, taking 11th place at almost the same speed as the previous year: 158 km/h (98.2 mph). Soon after, Hopkirk finished a steady fourth in the Bridgehampton 500-mile race in America behind three far lighter cars, a Porsche 904GTS and two Lotuses. The ex-Jacobs Midgets, which belonged to the factory, were also prepared for GT racing as works entries that year; one of the cars, driven by Hedges and Roger Mac, won its class at Sebring, and the other, with Hopkirk and Hedges at the wheel, finished 11th in the Targa Florio. Much to the corporation's surprise BMC found itself third in the GT constructors' world championship, so a more ambitious programme was planned for 1966 although the MGB was, by then, too slow to qualify at Le Mans.

The great road-racers

Three new cars were built and two of the old ones retained; they were all roadsters because, amazingly, the GT had not been homologated (or qualified) for international competition. Unfortunately, mechanical problems intervened in the first two events, the Monte Carlo Rally and Sebring. However, Syd Enever's son, Roger, took the place of the works cars in the Ilford Films 500 at Brands Hatch with the works development hack, beating all the Le Mans-style racing sports cars except a 7-litre AC Cobra and a Ford GT40!

He could not use one of the official works cars because they were away in Sicily for the Targa Florio. This was also an outstanding success for Abingdon as rally ace Timo Makinen, with circuit racer Rhodes, took the ex-Monte Carlo Rally car to a GT category win and ninth place overall. Hedges and John Handley were second in class with another works MGB which went on to win the GT category in the Spa 1000 kilometres race on the way back to Britain. These were really tough sports cars, driven down to the events by road, and it was hardly surprising that the Hedges car blew a water hose in the Nürburgring 1000 kilometres in Germany during a further detour on the long drive back from Sicily.

The Targa Florio car and Enever's hack – which had completed 10,000 miles at 160 km/h (100 mph) at Montlhéry as part of a Shell publicity exercise – were then entered in the 84-hour Marathon de la Route at the Nürburgring. This circuit race was officially a rally, a replacement for the Liège-Sofia-Liège event – a thinly disguised road race that had been upsetting holidaymakers and had been, in earlier form, a glorious proving ground for the Mark I Sprite. Both M.G.s suffered damage in crashes early on, but fought back to the head of the field. Hedges, with Julien Vernaeve, went on to win the event in a blaze of publicity, with Enever's car crashing again before retiring with a broken halfshaft. The battered cars were soon repaired, however, and went on to finish second and third in class behind a Porsche Carrera 6 in the Montlhéry 1000 kilometres race.

Meanwhile the development department at Abingdon had been busy with new models, the first of which, the Mark III Midget (and Mark IV Sprite), was introduced at the London Motor Show in October 1966. This was a more luxurious version of the Spridget with, among other fittings, a folding hood. The additional comfort was aimed mainly at the US market, but it was also important to make sure that the performance did not suffer because American cars were in the middle of a horsepower race at the time. So the heavier new Spridgets were fitted with a 1275 cc A-series engine based on that of the Mini-Cooper S,

raising their top speed slightly from 148 km/h (92 mph) to 150 km/h (93 mph) and improved acceleration marginally at the same time. These changes were particularly important because of improvements to Triumph's range of Spitfire-based sports cars, which now included the high-performance six-cylinder GT6.

The MGC

As sales of the larger and, it must be admitted, old-fashioned Austin-Healey 3000 declined, BMC asked Abingdon to save money by revising the MGB to accept the Big Healey's six-cylinder engine rather than develop a completely new model. As plenty of room had been left under the bonnet of the MGB at the design stage, it was possible to fit the Austin-Healey's C-series engine; the main problem was that it was too heavy.

However, Austin was reworking the engine in any case for a new saloon car, and said that the revised C-series engine would be far lighter, so Enever went ahead with adapting the MGB to take the new unit. It was then intended to badge-engineer the MGB as an Austin-Healey 1800, with the new car being marketed as the MGC and the Austin-Healey 3000 Mark IV. There were delays in completing the new C-series 3-litre engine and to Abingdon's dismay it turned out to be virtually the same weight as the old C-series unit because it incorporated seven main bearings instead of four. It also had a very conservative cylinder head design which limited power and revs: in fact, it was anything but a sports car engine. Enever had already redesigned the MGB's front suspension to use torsion bars rather than coil springs in a strengthened floorpan to accommodate the larger engine, but now he had to revise the settings hurriedly to cope with the extra weight. Inevitably the car could not be made to handle as well as an MGB, or an Austin-Healey 3000, and Donald Healey flatly refused to

ABOVE AND RIGHT *Although the long-nosed MGB finished 11th at Le Mans in 1965, it was also used for other events with standard bodywork, and it has been retained in that more practical form by Barry Sidery-Smith today. All the BMC Special Tuning parts on this car were available to customers.*

LEFT *John Thornley in retirement, refusing to be upstaged by either his dog or his MGB GT, registered, appropriately, MG 1. Despite his assertions to the contrary, he performed great feats of memory to help the author. Lest the purists howl, let it be pointed out that this car left the factory in 1973 with V8 road wheels and an early grille because of a temporary shortage of parts!*

RIGHT *Bill Nicholson's MGB leads Roger Enever in a works development hack MGB in the Ilford Films 500-mile race at Brands Hatch in 1966. Enever took third place and Nicholson seventh.*

lend his name to it. Nevertheless, BMC had to have a new 3-litre sports car to replace the existing Austin-Healey 3000, because it could not be modified sufficiently economically to meet new American safety regulations. Therefore the new car was introduced in July 1967 only as an M.G., in roadster and GT form.

The unfortunate MGC was immediately criticized by the press because of its nose-heavy handling and inability to perform as vigorously as the old Austin-Healey. In addition, it looked almost exactly the same as an MGB, except for odd protrusions such as a lump on the bonnet to clear the front carburettor. The result was that sales were far lower than expected. Nevertheless, because of its additional power and high top speed (193 km/h, 120 mph) and relaxed high-speed cruising ability, the MGC has since become something of a cult car with M.G. enthusiasts.

At the same time, the MGB was revised to accept a more modern all-synchromesh gearbox and the option of an automatic gearchange, which was expected to be very popular in America (the MGC incorporated this from the start). The interior was also revised along the lines of the MGC to meet the American safety regulations and a

MGC (1968)

ENGINE
Type	M.G. in-line, water-cooled
No. of cylinders	6
Bore/stroke mm	83 × 89
Displacement cc	2912
Valve operation	Overhead, pushrod
Sparkplugs per cyl.	1
Compression ratio	9:1
Induction	Two SU carburettors
BHP	145

DRIVE TRAIN
Clutch	Dry plate
Transmission	Four-speed manual, three-speed automatic, or manual and overdrive

CHASSIS
Frame	Unitary
Wheelbase mm	2311
Track – front mm	1245
Track – rear mm	1257
Suspension – front	Independent wishbone and torsion bar
Suspension – rear	Half-elliptic springs, live axle
Brakes	Discs front, drums rear
Tyre size – front	165 × 15
Tyre size – rear	165 × 15
Wheels	Wire spoke or steel disc

PERFORMANCE
Maximum speed	193 km/h (120 mph)
Acceleration	0-60 mph 10 sec
Fuel consumption	15.7 litres/100 km (18 mpg)
Number built	8999

BELOW *The MGC suffered an unfortunate battering from the Press, but it was, in fact, a very relaxed long-distance cruiser that deserved higher sales than it achieved. This 1968 roadster, restored by Derek and Pearl McGlen, was provided by Richard Tasker.*

US-specification engine was developed to meet emission regulations that were about to be introduced in 1968. The new model, which made its first appearance at the London Motor Show in October 1967, was subsequently known as the MGB Mark II.

Meanwhile, the competition department had built new cars for the 1967 season, including an MGB GT. Instead of using roadsters with hard tops, it was felt that there was more future in publicizing the standard shape in international GT racing, and a batch of competition MGC GT bodyshells was also ordered. The standard GT shell was very heavy, so they were built on a steel floorpan with an alloy superstructure. In fact, this was a difficult process, and there were delays, so the works MGB GT used a standard shell. This was prepared for the first big race of the season, at Sebring, with a 2004 cc B-series engine to run in the 2- to 3-litre class, because the Austin-Healey 3000, although still in production, had been eliminated by ever-tightening regulations. The MGB's engine was absolutely at the limit of its capacity, and no more could be extracted. The GT bodyshell had still not been homologated, so this near-standard car had to run as a prototype, and the Marathon-winning roadster qualified as a GT! In the event, both cars finished third in their class.

The MGC had not yet been announced when the Targa Florio was run, so the 2004 cc engine was fitted into the first of the lightweight MGC shells, because with its torsion-bar front suspension and wide wheels it had to run as a prototype. In this form, the new competition car finished ninth on the road, driven by Hopkirk and Makinen. Abingdon was then instructed to concentrate competition development on the Austin 1800 saloon now that had been fully badge-engineered throughout BMCs range, in addition to its Mini-Cooper S rally preparation, so the M.G.s were put aside.

The prototypes

A great deal of development time at the factory had been devoted to modifications to meet the American safety and environmental laws, in addition to the MGC, but Abingdon still managed to produce a prototype to replace both Spridget and MGB. This was a neat little open two-plus-two seater, code-named EX234, to accept either the A- or the B-series power units. With independent suspension on all four

ABOVE AND BELOW *The MGC also suffered from a lack of development by the works, even for international competition, but Abingdon's role was taken over by Bristol-based racer John Chatham who bought much of the stock when the factory abandoned racing in 1969. He built up an ultra-lightweight circuit racer, above, which is still one of the fastest M.G.s ever, and a road-racing version, below, which provided him with a top-level mount for the Targa Florio in 1970.*

wheels and a pleasing appearance, it could have been a winner as the MGD, had the parent company not been involved in what amounted to a takeover by the Leyland truck group.

BMC had merged with Jaguar to form British Motor Holdings in 1966, and then went on in 1968 to merge with Leyland (which also owned M.G.'s rival, Triumph). BMC, and subsequently BMH, had been having serious cash-flow problems with the popular family saloons, which meant that heavy investment for new sports cars such as the MGD was not available. And when Leyland's Donald Stokes took over as chairman and managing director of the new group, called the British Leyland Motor Corporation (BLMC), his natural inclination was towards the Triumph management and its range of sports cars, which needed replacement far more urgently than M.G.'s.

As part of the rationalization that took place at the time of British Leyland's formation, the Magnette was dropped in 1968 and the smaller M.G. saloon received the 1275 cc A-series engine, now known as the M.G. 1300. On the competition front, the MGC needed all the promotion it could get, so the Targa Florio lightweight prototype was rebuilt with a 3-litre engine for Sebring in 1968. This seven-bearing unit was highly experimental, with an alloy cylinder block as well as its alloy head, which had long been a feature of the earlier C-series engines used by competition Austin-Healeys. The idea was not only to reduce the overall weight of the racing MGC GT but also to make it handle as well as an MGB. The steel-bodied MGB GT was also prepared to run in the GT class at Sebring; it finished 18th overall, with the lightweight MGC (called a GTS by the works) taking 10th place overall and third in the prototype class behind the inevitable Porsches.

Abingdon continued to compete spasmodically during 1968; the GTS was joined by another to run in the Marathon de la Route. It seemed certain that the ex-Sebring GTS would have won the event from the Porsche opposition had brake wear not been miscalculated. In the end, seized callipers put it back into sixth place.

The two GTS cars and the MGB GT were sent to Sebring in 1969, but could manage only low placings against far more specialized opposition, before British Leyland decided to concentrate on rallies, and the remainder of its M.G. racing stock was sold to private entrants. There was little hope of success for these traditional sports cars now that they had to compete almost exclusively against more advanced mid-engined cars, and it seemed at that time that all sports cars would have to follow that trend.

The mid-engined configuration could endow a car with great traction and better handling in experienced hands, and potentially cost less to make with the elimination of the long drive line needed for a front-engined, rear-wheel drive car. Against those advantages had to be set the difficulties in giving such a vehicle the popular two-plus-two seating plan (the engine and transmission would effectively have to be in the back seat!) and other problems, such as restricted rearward visibility. Nevertheless, a prototype mid-engined car to use a new Austin E-series overhead camshaft power unit was prepared at Abingdon. This transverse engine and transmission, which had been introduced on the Austin Maxi, seemed ideal for the new car, designated ADO21 after its Austin Design Office number. It was an exciting new fixed-head coupé with a semi-wedge shape and de Dion rear suspension that effectively competed with EX234.

The Abingdon-designed car, EX234, had the advantage of being a convertible as well as using well-tried components; ADO21 was attractive because it represented the way in which sports car design trends were expected to go and it used a power unit which, although British Leyland recognized that it was far from perfect, had cost the organization a large amount of capital and needed using as much as possible to justify expenditure. In the event, the two designs competed against each other so vigorously that British Leyland's management decided to combine features of both ADO21's advanced wedge fixed-head profile with EX234's simple front-engined mechanical layout as a new Triumph!

In the meantime, the MGB was revised to meet increasingly stringent American emission regulations, with cosmetic changes only for the European cars in October 1969; these included a new black grille, chrome-plated wheels and Leyland badges on the wings, as the new group started a policy of promoting its corporate image rather than those of the individual marques.

It was during this period also that many of the old guard at Abingdon reached retirement age. The loss of Thornley in 1969 and Enever in 1971 was particularly deeply felt. However, the demise of the MGC in

1969 went virtually unlamented, although Abingdon still felt there was a market for a more potent sports car than the MGB. Some of Enever's last work included trying in the MGB the Daimler 2.5-litre V8 engine then being produced by the Jaguar division of British Leyland, but the unit Abingdon would really have liked, the all-alloy 3.5-litre Rover V8, was not available at that time because all supplies were needed for Rover saloons and Range-Rover production. The Healey contract with British Leyland also came to an end in 1971, and the Sprite variant of the small sports car was dropped soon after.

Triumph's new rival
Meanwhile, as British Leyland planned the new Triumph sports car, the MGB received further low-cost development to reach its Mark III form in May 1971. American export models had been fitted with progressively less powerful engines as emission regulations bit deeper, but, for the Mark III, the European cars were given a new big-valve

MGB GT V8 (1973)	
ENGINE	
Type	Rover V8, water-cooled
No. of cylinders	8
Bore/stroke mm	89 × 71
Displacement cc	3528
Valve operation	Overhead, hydraulic tappets, pushrods
Sparkplugs per cyl.	1
Compression ratio	8.25:1
Induction	Two SU carburettors
BHP	137
DRIVE TRAIN	
Clutch	Dry plate
Transmission	Four-speed manual overdrive
CHASSIS	
Frame	Unitary
Wheelbase mm	2311
Track – front mm	1245
Track – rear mm	1250
Suspension – front	Independent wishbone and coil
Suspension – rear	Half-elliptic springs, live axle
Brakes	Discs front, drums rear
Tyre size – front	175 × 14
Tyre size – rear	175 × 14
Wheels	Steel and alloy disc
PERFORMANCE	
Maximum speed	201 km/h (125 mph)
Acceleration	0-60 mph 8.6 sec
Fuel consumption	11.3 litres/100 km (25 mpg)
Number built	2591

The MGB GT, with a neat V8 installation, handled far better than the MGC and went even faster, but it came at the wrong time as the world was assailed by a fuel crisis. Like the MGC, it deserved to sell more, and enthusiasts are still building replicas today because they cannot buy new ones. A 1973 model provided by Barry Sidery-Smith.

cylinder head which improved performance marginally.

Huge overriders were fitted to US export cars during the next year to meet tougher crash regulations, and the option of automatic transmission was withdrawn through lack of demand. The main problem was that the B-series engine was not sufficiently potent to cope with the power-sapping demands of an automatic gearbox during years in which straight-line performance was becoming more and more important for the people who bought sports cars. This was especially evident when the B-series engine was fitted with the emission equipment demanded in the automatic's biggest potential market, America.

Between 1970 and 1972, a freelance tuner, Ken Costello, had been fitting Rover V8 engines to standard MGBs. It was a particularly successful conversion in that the 3528 cc Rover unit – which was by now readily available – weighed only about the same as the cast-iron B-series engine and fitted neatly under the bonnet to give a top speed of around 200 km/h (125 mph) with vastly improved acceleration.

This relatively cheap conversion received extensive publicity and British Leyland was stung into action to produce its own MGB V8, tooling for the stiffer and potentially more suitable MGC bodyshell having been scrapped in 1969. So they stopped supplies of new engines to Costello and authorized a hurried development programme at Abingdon. The main problems were that Abingdon considered the MGB roadster bodyshell was not really stiff enough to cope with the tremendous torque of the Rover engine. In addition, the factory felt that the MGB's manual gearbox had only a marginal capacity to absorb the torque for a prolonged period. Rover had just introduced a manual gearbox for the V8, but the company needed all its supplies for its own cars first.

However, the MGB GT bodyshell was strong enough to take the V8 engine and, despite Triumph's objections, development went ahead on that basis. The Triumph men did not like the idea of an MGB GT V8 because it would be potentially faster than their TR6 sports car and Stag tourer, and they were afraid that their sales would suffer badly as a result. They wanted British Leyland to drop the MGB GT in any case because the new TR7 sports car was intended as a hard top. They were not too concerned about the four-cylinder MGB roadster because it was anticipated that American crash regulations would outlaw open cars by 1975, and it would not be worth making an open model for the European market alone.

But Stokes said that if Costello could make money from an MGB V8, despite paying the full price for the extra components and having to discard the existing engine, then Leyland should be able to do even better. So he gave Abingdon the go-ahead to produce the MGB GT V8 with an MGC gearbox on a short-term basis until Triumph could introduce a V8 version of the TR7. This new car, in four-cylinder, or in eight-cylinder form, could be badge-engineered as an M.G. in any case.

The tough new world
It was in this difficult political atmosphere that the MGB GT V8 was introduced in August 1973. Sadly, it ran into trouble straight away. Within two months Israel was at war with the Arabs and soon after the West experienced its first fuel crisis since 1956. An 80 km/h (50 mph) speed limit was imposed in Britain and everyone's attention turned from high performance to ultimate economy, and thirsty V8s became plain unfashionable. Another factor that operated against the MGB GT V8 was that British Leyland dealers in America, who had to sell the Stag and Jaguar's ageing E type, were against it. As a result, left-hand-drive versions of the MGB GT V8 did not progress beyond the prototype stage, and the model was denied even the European market. Yet another factor that contributed to the MGB GT V8's problems was that the Ford Capri was already well established on the British market. It was readily available with a variety of engines up to 3 litres and had a far superior ride and bigger back seats. In fact, had Thornley and Enever been given their head in the early 1960s, they would have chosen to produce a car like the Capri, with larger rear seats, a wide selection of engines, and a much lighter bodyshell made possible by the use of the roof as a stressed member. So the potential saviour of the M.G. range was to fight and lose an uphill sales battle.

By 1975, the American market was becoming really tough, as British Leyland and many other manufacturers had anticipated, although their worst fears that open cars would be banned were not realized. Some manufacturers, such as Porsche, made an outstanding success of developing their range to pass the new crash regulations, which stipulated that the car must be capable of taking a blow from a massive concrete block at 8 km/h (5 mph) without damage to safety-related items such as the lighting. In addition, bumpers had to be of a standard height, which in the case of the low-slung M.G.s meant raising them level with those on an average lumbering American saloon. Jaguar had

Midget (1978)	
ENGINE	
Type	Triumph in-line, water-cooled
No. of cylinders	4
Bore/stroke mm	74 × 87.5
Displacement cc	1493
Valve operation	Overhead, pushrod
Sparkplugs per cyl.	1
Compression ratio	9:1
Induction	Two SU carburettors
BHP	66
DRIVE TRAIN	
Clutch	Dry plate
Transmission	Four-speed manual
CHASSIS	
Frame	Unitary
Wheelbase mm	2030
Track – front mm	1160
Track – rear mm	1140
Suspension – front	Independent wishbone and coil
Suspension – rear	Half-elliptic springs, live axle
Brakes	Discs front, drums rear
Tyre size – front	145 × 13
Tyre size – rear	145 × 13
Wheels	Wire spoke or steel disc
PERFORMANCE	
Maximum speed	150 km/h (93 mph)
Acceleration	0-60 mph 11.9 sec
Fuel consumption	10.46 litres/100 km (27 mpg)
Number built	88,906

ABOVE AND RIGHT *The M.G. Midget eventually received a 1500 cc engine from the rival Triumph Spitfire to keep up its performance. A 1978 model provided by Alan Baker.*

LEFT *The MGB stayed in production little altered for 18 years. A 1980 roadster provided by Performance Cars Ltd.*

to drop its E type as a result, but M.G. just scraped through by reworking the MGB and Midget with massive rubberized bumpers. Insufficient capital was available for a new floorpan because all the British Leyland cash available for sports cars was going into TR7 development. So the M.G.'s suspension had to be jacked up to increase the ride height and thus the bumper height. The Midget was not very badly affected by these changes, and even gained in performance. This was because it was given the 1491 cc four-cylinder engine used in the rival Triumph Spitfire, which could cope better with the strangulation of the American emission laws. But there was no such convenient unit for the MGB, and therefore its performance suffered from the extra weight of the new bumpers, and the handling deteriorated because of the increased ride height.

Sales did not suffer, however, because the M.G.s were among the few open sports cars that survived this traumatic year. The way that the MGB maintained its total sales also emphasized the regard in which

the marque was held in America. The Triumph lobby within British Leyland had persuaded top management to drop the MGB GT from the American market to give a clear field for the TR7 when it was introduced for export only in January 1975. British Leyland felt, quite naturally, that having sunk so much money into the TR7 it should be promoted as much as possible. So the company's pricing policies were also heavily weighted in favour of the TR7 against the M.G. But the M.G. was a dependable open car and the TR7, with its controversial wedge shape and its teething troubles, fared badly against the MGB.

And so the MGB and Midget soldiered on until 1980 (the V8 was dropped in 1976), numerous detail changes being incorporated to improve handling and meet more stringent European regulations. But not even Abingdon could carry on selling an antique in numbers sufficient to keep one factory going as British Leyland floundered under increasingly severe cash problems. The TR7 was not a sales success and there was insufficient cash to design and develop a new sports car.

MG Metro (1982)

ENGINE

Type	M.G. in-line, water-cooled
No. of cylinders	4
Bore/stroke mm	71 × 81
Displacement cc	1275
Valve operation	Overhead, pushrod
Sparkplugs per cyl.	1
Compression ratio	10.5:1
Induction	One SU carburettor
BHP	72

DRIVE TRAIN

Clutch	Dry plate
Transmission	Four-speed manual

CHASSIS

Frame	Unitary
Wheelbase mm	2251
Track – front mm	1274
Track – rear mm	1274
Suspension – front	Independent unequal length links, Hydragas spring
Suspension – rear	Independent trailing arms, Hydragas spring
Brakes	Discs front, drums rear
Tyre size – front	155/70 × 12
Tyre size – rear	155/70 × 12
Wheels	Alloy disc

PERFORMANCE

Maximum speed	142 km/h (88 mph)
Acceleration	0-60 mph 10.9 sec
Fuel consumption	8.97 litres/100 km (31.5 mpg)
Number built	Still in production

The M.G. marque had really come full circle with the introduction of the MG Metro in May 1982, for the new car was a more attractive and sportier version of a basic family vehicle. Provided by BL Cars Limited.

Eventually Abingdon had to close altogether in 1980, as British Leyland drew in its horns. The tragedy was made even worse when it was realized that the superbly loyal workforce had hardly ever had a strike, whereas there had been serious problems in this area with TR7 production. What was more, because of the frugal way in which Abingdon was run, it cost less to make a car there than at any other British Leyland factory. Even so, BL claimed it was losing hundreds of pounds on every M.G. sold in the USA and eventually, after an unsuccessful attempt to rescue Abingdon by the small specialist car maker, Aston Martin, the famous M.G. factory was closed.

However, British Leyland refused to sell the legendary name of M.G., saving it for a high-performance version of the new car it saw as its salvation, the Metro. With a 1300 cc engine based on the A-series unit, the light new four-seater MG Metro was launched in May 1982. It was capable of 142 km/h (88 mph) – making it one of the fastest-ever M.G. production saloons – and invited comparison with the Mini-Cooper of old. It was entirely a product of Longbridge, but was welcomed by M.G. enthusiasts who recognized it as a modern sports car with excellent handling and economy. The days of the traditional open sports car might be over for a while, but an even faster turbocharged Metro was waiting in the wings. This exciting new car was introduced at the British Motor Show in October 1982 as a result of a joint development exercise with the British high-performance car maker, Lotus. This small specialist manufacturer already boasted one of the finest turbocharged engines available, installed in the very fast Esprit Turbo.

It was the basis of this technology that gave the MG Metro Turbo a power output of 93 bhp at 6130 rpm with excellent torque of 116 Nm (85 lbf ft) at 2650 rpm. It was enough to give the new car a maximum speed of 180 km/h (112 mph) with a 9.9-second 0-97 km/h (0-60 mph) acceleration time. During the next year, another MG joined the Metros, an upmarket 102 bhp Weber-carburettor version of BL's new medium-sized saloon, the Maestro. The Maestros were aimed at taking 25 per cent of the British family car market. This was followed in April 1984 by a high-performance, 2-litre M.G. version of BL's large saloon, the Montego, to complete the range, giving a line-up of three M.G.s on the market.

With the Metro car, British Leyland could re-enter international competition in the top echelons of circuit racing and rallying. It could be seen that the marque M.G. had come full circle from the very first improved Morris models to the latest improved saloons.

LEFT *Powerhouse of the new MG Metro Turbo (the turbocharger is situated under the carburettor). This car could be readily distinguished by bold Turbo flashes on the side, front spoiler and new wheels. Provided by BL Cars Limited.*

BELOW *The new MG high-performance version of BL's Maestro saloon, showing similar upmarket trim to the MG Metros.*

Index

Acknowledgements

The publishers wish to thank the following organizations and individuals for their kind permission to reproduce the photographs in this book:

Austin Rover Group 79 below, BL Heritage Limited 6-7, 10, 16-17, 20, 36, 36-7, 38; Neill Bruce 28; LAT Photographic 52, 65, 69, 71.

Special Photography:
Ian Dawson, 1, 2-3, 4-5, 6, 11, 12-13, 14-15, 16, 18-19, 21, 24, 25, 26, 27, 28, 29, 30-31, 34-5, 36-7, 42, 43, 56, 58-9, 60-61, 64, 66-7, 68-9, 70-71, 72-3, 74, 76-7, 78-9

Chris Linton 8-9, 10, 13, 16-17, 22-3, 32, 38-9, 40, 41, 44, 45-6, 47, 48-9, 52, 53, 54-5, 57, 62-3, 68, 70, 75.

In addition, the publishers would like to thank the following for their valuable assistance on this book: John Thornley, the M.G. Car Club (Peter Tipton), the M.G. Owner's Club (Roche Bentley), BL Cars Limited (Clive Richardson), BL Heritage Limited, J. Alastair B. Naylor of Naylor Brothers, and Simon J. Robinson.

Thanks are also due to the owners who kindly allowed their cars to be photographed.